MORE PRAISE FOR *No Land's Man*

"I was enthralled. . . . Mandvi writes beautifully and comedically about his life, with wonderful dialogue and revealing detail, reminiscent of David Sedaris."
—JONATHAN AMES, author of *Wake Up, Sir!*

"Aasif is my favorite Indo-Muslim-British-American *Daily Show* correspondent ever. I loved *No Land's Man*!"
—JIM GAFFIGAN, author of *Dad Is Fat* and *Food: A Love Story*

"It always bothered me that Aasif was more than merely funny—he's also a great actor. Now I've learned he's an amazing storyteller as well, and I am furious . . . but also grateful. Aasif's movement between cultures and genres is what makes him and his story singularly funny, poignant, and essential."
—JOHN HODGMAN, author of *The Areas of My Expertise* and *More Information Than You Require*

"We need more books like this—or rather, we need to read more books like this—in order to understand the fundamental humanity that we all share, regardless of skin color."
—Daily Kos

"A lighthearted but heartfelt portrait of Mandvi's childhood and his struggles to come to terms with his rather complicated life."
—*The Boston Globe*

NO LAND'S MAN

by

AASIF MANDVI

CHRONICLE BOOKS
SAN FRANCISCO

DISCLAIMER: Although the stories in this book are based on true events, the specific circumstances are often a blend of fact and imagination. Some of the names, identifying characteristics, and circumstances have been changed . . . sometimes for the better, but that's just my opinion.

First Chronicle Books LLC paperback edition published in 2015. Originally published in hardcover in 2014 by Chronicle Books LLC.

Library of Congress Cataloging-in-Publication Data available.
ISBN: 978-1-4521-4532-7

Manufactured in China.

Cover design by Gregg Kulick and Neil Egan
Book design by Neil Egan
Cover Illustration by Jim Tierney

10 9 8 7 6 5 4 3 2 1

Chronicle Books LLC
680 Second Street
San Francisco, California 94107
www.chroniclebooks.com

For my mother Fatima, who encouraged me to day dream
Also for Hakim and Shabana

CONTENTS

Part I

WELCOME HOME: THE RETURN

MY FAMILY LEFT the Northern English textile factory town of Bradford and moved to America in the early 1980s when I was sixteen years old. It happened so fast that I never really had a chance to say a proper goodbye to the place where I spent my childhood. As a teenager you tend to focus on the future rather than the past, and because my life after college and in New York was busy and full, I never had a desire to return. This actually might not come as a surprise to anyone who has ever lived in Bradford, for until my parents saved up enough to move us to the suburbs, we lived against the backdrop of factories, mills, graffiti-ridden tenement buildings, and run-down council estates. I remember the entire city looking like it was covered in soot.

However, sixteen years later, now living in New York and working as an actor, I had recently closed a successful run of my one-man show *Sakina's Restaurant*[1], which I had written and per-

1. The play *Sakina's Restaurant* was originally directed and developed by Kim Hughes.

formed at the American Place Theater in New York City after several years of development. The play was critically well received and it ran for almost six months in the tiny black box theater below 46th Street. It was the culmination of several years of hard work for me, with write-ups in the *New York Times* and movie directors and VIP's coming to see me perform. It was my first brush with success in a business that I had been struggling to make it in for almost a decade.

Through the process of workshopping the play, performing, and rewriting it, I managed to excavate what I thought was the story of my immigrant experience. As solo shows often are, it was a personal and cathartic performance and became a way for me to examine how my own issues of identity and dislocation had affected me.

As I performed the play every night, I had the sense that I had uncovered something that had lain dormant in me for a long time and I could not put it back to sleep. The play that I thought would put the pieces of my dislocated identity together, actually just shone a spotlight on the pieces that were missing and I realized after some time of denying it, that those pieces were back in Bradford.

I began to feel nostalgic for the city of my childhood. I thought about returning to the house that I grew up in, my middle school and boarding school, the reservoir where I went sledding as a child, my Dad's corner shop and the makeshift little children's theater where I first discovered my love of being a performer. This feeling came about suddenly and I couldn't really understand it, or afford it, honestly. Traveling to England is expensive for anyone, especially someone making an off-Broadway theater actor's salary.

My opportunity to return presented itself serendipitously a few months later.

After one of the performances, a screenwriter friend mentioned my show to the famed Indian film director Shekhar Kapur. Shekhar and I became friends and for a while thereafter he would buy me lunch whenever he was in New York. He also happened to be working with Andrew Lloyd Webber on what would later become the musical *Bombay Dreams*. During one of our lunches in New York he mentioned Sydmonton, a festival that Andrew put on every year at his country estate. Shekhar thought my show would be perfect for the festival and he told me that if I came out to England, he would set up a meeting. "It would be a wonderful addition and I'm sure Andrew would be very excited," he said.

As I left the restaurant I marveled at the strange circumstance that was about to accompany my return to England. It felt somehow fated. I didn't sing and the only Webber Musical I had ever seen was *Jesus Christ Superstar* so being invited back to England in this manner felt akin to being invited to Rome to meet with the Pope. You kind of have to stop making excuses and just go. Returning to England in this way also felt like a tremendous accomplishment. It would be a triumphant return, I thought! The little Indian kid from Bradford who was called a wog and chased home from the bus stop every night returning to perform his "toast of New York" play about being an Indian immigrant for the British aristocracy. I was pretty chuffed with myself as I walked around my apartment for several days singing, "Aasif Mandvi, Superstaaaaar! I'm going to be best friends with Lloyd Webbaaaar!"

Several weeks later I found myself sitting in the offices of The Really Useful Group, Andrew Lloyd Webber's headquarters in London. His associate finally came back into the office with an apologetic look on his face.

"I am so terribly sorry," he said, "but Andrew has to leave. He feels dreadful for making you wait, but something has come up and he has to dash. When do you leave to go back to New York?"

"The day after tomorrow," I said, standing up and gathering my things.

"Oh, that's too bad," he said as he led me to the door. "He has time next week but you won't be here."

I could tell from his tone that he had more important things on his plate than talking to some unknown actor from New York.

"Hope this wasn't the only reason you came over to England" he said.

"No. No, of course not," I said, somewhat unconvincingly. "I actually grew up in Bradford so I'm going to visit my hometown."

"Bradford," he said, "huh? I've never been."

There was an awkward pause after which he said, "Well, have a great trip, and let's schedule it for another time, when you are back in the UK."

"I will," I said, knowing that would never happen.

He shook my hand and apologized again as he showed me the stairs to the street.

I went back to my bed and breakfast, packed my bags, and made my way to Kings Cross Station.

"The next train to Bradford," I said to the lady at the ticket booth.

"Good curry in Bradford," she replied.

"I know, I grew up there."

"Yeah, that's what I thought," she said as she smacked her gum and pulled out a train schedule. "Bradford is full of your kind."

"My kind?" I repeated tentatively, hoping she meant Bradford was full of strikingly handsome men.

"Yeah, you know," she said nodding towards me. "Asians. Lots of Asians in Bradford."

"Well, it's been a long time," I replied, not knowing what else to say.

"Homesick, then, are you?" she asked.

"Yes, something like that," I replied, smiling. "I suppose I'm going to take a trip down memory lane."

She smiled back and then looked pensive for a moment.

"I'm not sure I can recommend that," she said as she handed me the train schedule. "Dangerous business, that is."

"I suppose it can be," I said as I dropped a few pounds under the window.

"Good luck," she said. "I hope you find whatever you're looking for."

BETTER THAN FONZ

"DR. *ZHIVAGO.* IT CHANGED MY LIFE."

I spoke so quietly I don't think he even heard me. But he was probably used to that. Wherever he went, I imagined, gasps of recognition followed, along with the sounds of people whispering his name or the titles of the movies he'd starred in. I didn't care about them. Those people may have been fans, maybe wanting his autograph or to have their picture taken with him, but for me it was much more than that. I wasn't just an admirer or a sycophant, someone who just wanted to flatter him because he was a big star. I didn't even really want to engage him in a conversation about his career or about the challenges of working in Hollywood, blah blah blah. . . . He was so much more than that to me.

The best way to describe the way I felt about him would be to call it familial, like I was his offspring, metaphorically speaking, much the way Sidney Poitier was like a father figure to so many African-American actors. He had sown the seeds for myself and other brown actors hoping to work in Hollywood.

I said it again, a little louder and clearer this time, with confidence, supporting my voice with my diaphragm like I had been taught in acting school. I could feel my voice rising above the din of the Manhattan rooftop bar where I was serving drinks.

"*Dr. Zhivago*. It changed my life."

I spoke with an assurance I didn't quite feel. He turned to me, finally realizing that a young waiter was addressing him, saying something other than "May I get you another?" He looked at me sharply, noting my timid, perhaps even dimwitted expression. I had surprised myself by my boldness, and apparently I had surprised him, too. The problem now, I realized, was that I had no plan of action for the moment after contact was made. And contact had been made. A smile began to form on his mouth, in his eyes, and even his cheekbones. I was a waiter who had interrupted the conversation of a celebrity VIP guest, which was a huge no-no. I could very easily be fired for my brazenness, but strangely, I didn't care. I had seized the moment. I had connected with one of my idols. But what should I say or do next? I grinned like an idiot, unable to leave, unable to stay.

My path to this awkward and fumbling moment began years earlier. In the summer of 1977, when I was eleven years old, I decided I was going to become an actor. I confided my plans to my mother one day after watching an episode of *Happy Days*, the one where Fonzie tries to be a normal person like Richie Cunningham and fails miserably. I related to Fonzie not because of his cool factor, which he obviously had in abundance, but because his real name was Arthur Fonzarelli, which I knew instinctively, even as a naive eleven-year-old, was a name almost as unusual and uncool as my name, Asif Mandviwala.[2] Even with this liability, Arthur Fonzarelli was still the epitome of coolness. All it took was that observation, along with

---

2. My parents named me Asif, which unbeknownst to them at the time, means "sorry" in Arabic. I lived with this apology of a name until my mother finally discovered that if you just add an extra "a," slightly changing the pronunciation, it becomes "the chaos of a big wind."

a belief that TV acting involved no more than putting on a leather jacket and riding a motorcycle around Milwaukee, Wisconsin, to persuade me that Asif Mandviwala was destined to become the Monz.

As I shared my thinking with my mother, she lay back on the couch and applied an ice bag to her forehead. Her eyes closed, she remained very quiet. My mother suffered from recurring migraines, which usually required that I rub Tiger Balm on her forehead just at the moment I was about to go and ride my bike. This particular headache, though, was no doubt brought on by the fact that my friend Sean and I had spent the entire morning driving tanks through the dining room, quite successfully defending our modest three-bedroom bungalow from a river of molten lava, an alien invasion, and three hundred and thirty-two tiny green soldiers. As a warrior returning from battle, and a Monz-to-be, I needed attention from my mother, so migraine be damned, I yelled at the top of my lungs.

"MA! I WANT TO BE AN ACTOR!"

Now, my mother has only ever said two things to me as a child that I didn't understand. The first was, "Why do you have to go out to play?" and the second was that afternoon, when she sat up, opened her eyes, and while sounding (and some would say even looking) remarkably like Yoda, she uttered the following words: "Omar Sharif–like actor?"

I don't know what I had hoped for in response, but it certainly wasn't that. I had never heard of Omar Sharif. I assumed he was someone my parents knew, most likely the son of some other Indian family.

My parents were always comparing my behavior and successes or lack thereof to the behavior and successes of children of other

Indian families we knew. "Sunil doesn't talk to his mother that way," they would comment. It was the perfect parental inadequacy monitor that Indian parents could train on their kids whenever they were feeling pretty good about themselves, guaranteed to take the wind out of their sails. If I brought home Bs on my report card, Alpana was certain to bring home As. If I took out the garbage for my mother, I found out that Raj didn't have to be told, he just did it. If I helped my dad clean the garage, Milan, I was reminded, had cleaned the garage when his parents were on vacation so that it would be a surprise for them when they returned. So naturally I assumed that once again, my mother was resorting to inadequacy tactics by bringing up this overachieving Omar Sharif kid who had no doubt played the flute or recited a poem at some cheesy local Indian community talent contest.

This time, I thought to myself, it's not going to work. My mother would not inadequate my parade.

"I hate that kid!" I shouted.

My mother just smiled sweetly at me and stroked my hair while my eyes burned from the reeking Tiger Balm she'd smeared across her forehead.

"You don't know him," she whispered. "But if you want to be an actor, you should try and be like him."

"No, Ma, I want to be like the Fonz," I declared. For emphasis I put my thumbs at right angles and with the deepest, sexiest voice an eleven-year-old boy could muster while wearing red polyester shorts and a turtleneck, I delivered Fonzie's signature of coolness.

"Heeeeey . . ." I said. It was a long drawn out *hey* just like Fonzie's. I held it for a good ten seconds, just to the point of possibly needing to use my asthma inhaler if I continued much longer. When

I was done, my mother was at first silent. Then suddenly, she burst into a fit of laughter. Again, that wasn't the reaction I'd expected from her. I guess I'd hoped she would be impressed, even astonished, by my dead-on Fonzie impersonation. Instead, she couldn't stop laughing, as if she had never seen anything funnier. I waited for her to collect herself, to dry the tears of laughter that were running down her cheeks, and notice my piqued expression, which she finally did. Taking my face in her hands, she then said something that haunted me for the next several months.

"Omar Sharif is better than Fonz," she observed knowingly.

What? Had my mother even watched *Happy Days*? No one was better than the Fonz, especially not this stupid Omar Sharif kid. Was she out of her mind?

For the next several months, the name Omar Sharif kept popping up. He seemed to be everywhere, upstaging me and my brand-new determination to be an actor. Between deep breathing exercises, I proudly announced to my asthma doctor that I had decided to become an actor. Before my father could get out the words that were on the tip of his tongue whenever I mentioned my desire to follow in Fonzie's footsteps—"My son will go to medical school and become a doctor"—my friendly Indian doctor perked up while removing his stethoscope from my chest.

"You want to be an actor, is it?" He asked. "Omar Sharif–like actor?"

Again with this Omar Sharif! Before I even had the chance to stick out my thumbs and impress them both, I was being ushered out the door. I was devastated. Why did everyone think this Omar Sharif kid was so great? Why didn't my dad and my doctor understand? The bus driver, the woman at the grocery store, my neighbor, the milkman, even the man who came to inspect our gas meter all seemed to love Omar Sharif.

After hearing about my Fonzie dreams, the gas guy told me the story of how his brother had met Henry Winkler getting out of a taxi in New York. I was riveted by his story until my mother ruined it by interjecting that her son would not be an actor like Henry Winkler, but instead like Omar Sharif. In response, the gas meter inspector almost cracked his skull on the pipes under our sink when he straightened up and declared, "Omar Sharif! I love Omar Sharif!"

Since I was way too young to hire a private investigator, and this was before the internet, there was no way for me to find out on my own who Omar Sharif was. I was afraid to even ask about him, fearing that I might discover he really was as handsome and talented as everyone thought, at which point my jealousy would know no bounds, and my fragile dream of becoming an actor would be forever punctured and deflated. I couldn't risk that, so instead I comforted myself with fantasies of us confronting each other on the playground, where I would punch him in the nose so hard that he would run home crying. No doubt Omar was fat from stuffing his face with sweets all day, but still arrogant because inexplicably everyone seemed to love him despite his grotesque obesity. One day I would triumph over Omar Sharif.

A few months later, on Christmas Eve, we were at the home of another Indian family, with whom my parents played cards every Sunday. The living room of the tiny house was packed with brown faces, aunts and uncles from four or maybe ten or so different families and their kids, all gathered around one tiny television set. It was time for the main event, the BBC movie of the night. That night, there was an excitement and anticipation in the air that I had not noticed when we had watched movies together before. The MGM lion roared, and the music began to crescendo. My mother passed around napkins and Indian snacks. I sat in front of the screen sullenly, having been dragged up from the basement, away from Anil's Formula One race car tracks where for once I'd actually been winning. As the BBC announcer introduced the movie for the evening and announced the next few words, something happened inside my head. It was not unlike when Roy Scheider finally sees the shark on that crowded Long Island beach in the movie *Jaws*, a technique I believe was invented by Spielberg and adopted by my mind's eye for this momentous occasion. My consciousness dollied backward while the focus zoomed forward as I heard the words "*Dr. Zhivago*, starring Omar Sharif."

At first I was stunned. I thought I must have misheard, but after the announcer talked a little about the director and the making of the film, I heard it again. "*Dr. Zhivago*, starring Omar Sharif." Are you kidding me? I thought. You have got to be kidding me! But this was clearly no joke. The minute the movie began I stood up as if I was about to confront Omar Sharif with that long-awaited punch in the nose he so richly deserved. After a few minutes, my vision returned to normal and I watched the film, finally beginning to understand what everyone had been talking about when they said the name Omar Sharif.

That night, as the aunties served up bowls of bhel puri and chaklis and some uncles passed out on the sofa while others stayed up smoking cigars and playing gin rummy on a blanket laid out on the floor, I sat rapt in front of the television. I was not watching a movie called *Dr. Zhivago*, an epic about love, war, and revolution; I was watching my own dream come to life, in the form of a man whose face looked like no other lead actor I had ever seen in an English-language film. This man was not playing a servant or a savage like in Tarzan movies. He wasn't Gunga Din or Tonto or a Bedouin. This man was the epitome of a gentleman, albeit a brown gentleman, who spoke smoothly before kissing the beautiful, blonde, white Julie Christie. My mother was right. Omar Sharif was better than Fonz.

Many years later I was a young twenty-something actor who had just arrived in New York City, carrying my Screen Actors Guild card in my back pocket, standing face-to-face with that same brown gentleman who had somehow helped make my own dream possible.

"*Dr. Zhivago*. It changed my life," I repeated once more.

As I stood there not knowing what more to say, enveloped by the din of a Manhattan rooftop cocktail lounge, Omar Sharif smiled back at me. Nodding in recognition, almost familiarly, he leaned in to me and whispered, "Really? Mine, too."

CURRY POT COWBOY

I WAS NINE YEARS OLD WHEN I STARTED at the Rose Bank School for Boys and Girls, nestled deep in the heart of the English countryside. I mostly remember being there in the autumn, specifically during that particular kind of English autumn that one reads about in James Herriot books like *All Creatures Great and Small* or sees in the background of Merchant/Ivory films. I remember green hills, gray factories, and the sound of golden crispy wafer-like leaves crunching under my feet as I walked to school.

We were all dressed identically in maroon blazers and emblemed caps, gray shorts, and neatly-polished brown or black shoes. As we carried our shiny leather satchels filled with schoolbooks and homework for Latin, French, maths, and science up the school driveway, it was clear to anyone who saw us that we were England's future. We would gather every morning for assembly, during which our high-pitched, well-behaved voices would rise angelically over the Pennine hills and float through the crisp North Yorkshire air as we sang our hymns.

Jesus wants me for a sunbeam,
to shine for him each daaaaay,
In every way try to pleeeease him,
at home, at school, at plaaaaaay.

Being groomed for grammar school, we were mostly the children of bankers, lawyers, and doctors, all benefitting from the upper-middle-class privileges of private school. We imagined ourselves to be Wendy and Michael before they were visited by the infamous shadow of Peter Pan. We devoured Enid Blyton and Roald Dahl. We watched *Black Beauty* and *Blue Peter* on television. We ate cheese on toast and chased each other around at recess playing British bulldogs charge.[3]

However, as much as we may have dressed alike, talked alike, and played the same games, I am pretty sure I was the only student at Rose Bank School for Boys and Girls whose parents were shopkeepers and whose nickname was "Curry Pot." Due to my strict fish-and-chips upbringing, I had never actually seen a curry pot, and to be honest, I didn't even know if there was such a thing. If it did exist I imagined it must look a great deal like a chubby nine-year-old Indian boy. One who couldn't play football, always came home with a bloody nose on Fridays (courtesy of Mark Delancy), and once during arithmetic (much to the amusement of the entire class) had become tongue-tied and crumbled under the pressure of asking Judy Seaver if he could simply borrow her pencil.

There were many good reasons for me to be nervous around Judy Seaver. First of all, she was the most beautiful girl in our school . . . and maybe the entire world. Second, whereas I was "Curry Pot," Judy was "Maid Marian." Third, back when I was eight and Judy was eight and three-quarters I had embarrassed myself by making an attempt to engage her in conversation, emboldened by the fact that I was convinced she had smiled at me. I was wrong. Me rambling like an idiot to the back of Judy Seaver's head was the sum

3. The British version of tag.

total of our relationship, until the autumn of 1975, when something remarkable happened.

Rose Bank School for Boys and Girls was a seriously atypical small English private school run by Mr. and Mrs. Davis, an always grumpy and slightly loony husband-and-wife teaching team. The school actually existed inside their three-story home. Educating a total of about thirty students from ages five to eleven, the couple lived upstairs while classes were conducted downstairs in their living room and parlor, perfectly furnished with desks and chalkboards. The backyard doubled as our playground, morning assembly was held in the piano room, which doubled as the cafeteria, and P.E. was down in the cellar.

It was in that very same cellar that the remarkable event occurred. It was on a Tuesday during recess between arithmetic and P.E. that Mark Delancy discovered the mattress down in the cellar. The mattress! The other kids came running in as he pulled it out from behind an old armoire that the Davises were no doubt going to send to the rubbish heap. Now, to the jaded adult eye, the mattress would no doubt have been viewed as a flea-ridden excuse for a bonfire, but to Mark Delancy and the rest of our class, that dirty old mattress held the potential for a grand adventure.

As we all discussed what that adventure could possibly be, Mark Delancy looked me in the eye while I stood smiling underneath the cellar window and suggested what he considered would be the best and most fun use of the mattress. Mark Delancy first suggested most things that the other kids would then carry out, especially when those suggestions started, as they often did, with the phrase *Why don't we get Curry Pot to . . .* "hold his breath," "eat snot," "make himself puke," "look up Mrs. Davis's skirt," "steal a butter knife," "hold this frog," and now:

". . . kiss Judy on top of the mattress?!"

"What?" I gasped, as my smile disappeared and my eyes popped open wide.

Just hearing the words made my blood go cold. I stole a glance at Judy Seaver, whose face was red with embarrassment. I desperately wanted to articulate my objection to the idea and save us both from public humiliation but all I could manage to do was look dumbfounded and utter the word *what* over and over again. While I remained tongue-tied, the other kids immediately picked up on Mark Delancy's scheme and began urging me on. The same mob mentality that led to so many innocents in ancient times being sacrificed before the gods was now chanting for my head or worse, my irrevocable shame in front of a girl I secretly massively adored. The motley crew of well-groomed, otherwise well-behaved little English school children began to chant, "Judy kiss the Curry Pot, Judy kiss the Curry Pot, Judy kiss the Curry Pot."

So there it was. It had been decreed by the masses and now seemed inevitable. I did not have the character or the fortitude to stand up for Judy and myself against a cellar full of bloodthirsty schoolchildren. Judy looked like she was about to cry as we were led to our execution . . . I mean the mattress. I felt responsible for her humiliation as well as mine. I was used to taunts and teasing, but it seemed hugely unfair that someone as beautiful and popular as Judy should have to be subjected to this kind of experience.

It probably goes without saying that I had never kissed a girl on the lips before. I'd never even practiced. I'd thought that one probably wouldn't have to deal with that level of trauma until they were at least twenty-five years old. But here I was at nine years old, being folded into a doubled up mattress like the contents of a pita wrap with the girl of my dreams, while seventeen children and Mark Delancy pressed their bodies down on top of us so that even if it meant that our very breath would be snuffed out of us, the suffocation would at least happen with our lips pressed firmly against each other's.

Above our heads the chant of "Judy kiss the Curry Pot" was getting louder and louder. We could hear our classmates laughing and grunting, fighting each other for the sweet spot, the exact right location from which they could peek through the crease where the mattress folded together. Mark Delancy pushed everyone aside since he was the biggest and strongest of the group and since it had been his idea. Clearly he deserved the bird's-eye view.

Judy smelled clean like a girl. Her cheek was smooth and powdery against mine, her brown hair was in my mouth, our arms were contorted into each other's ribs and stomachs, and her breath smelled warm and sugary. In the time I had known her, Judy had never once spoken to me and, although I didn't know it at the time, she never would again. But on that day, during those few brief seconds we shared in the mattress, she did.

"Hello," she said.

"Hello," I replied.

I was just about to continue by apologizing for all this and tell her that of course we didn't have to kiss when something miraculous happened. Judy kissed me. It happened quite suddenly and it was most certainly deliberate. She looked me in the eye, smiled, and kissed me. As we kissed she held on to me for dear life, as if we were taking off together in a rocket ship, or going down together in a plane crash. (I couldn't tell which.) Our lips were locked and our faces were smashed together so hard that our teeth ached. I squeezed my eyes shut so tight to keep out the embarrassment that my eyeballs even began to hurt.

High above we could hear the laughter and the roar of the other children as they relentlessly chanted "Kiss, kiss, kiss." Our kiss seemed to last forever, going on and on and on! As more and more children jumped on top of the mattress insisting that their voyeurism be satisfied, we became locked together, unable to move. As we gave in to our predicament, our desperate kiss seemed to grow into something different. However it had started and whatever the fallout would be afterwards, we were kissing each other. Really kissing each other. Our mouths went from tense to soft, our breathing became deeper and our bodies became relaxed and we found ourselves no longer entangled but rather embracing each other. We were sharing a simultaneously humiliating and beautiful moment. We were together and everything else seemed to disappear: the mattress, the mocking children, the Rose Bank School for Boys and Girls, they all suddenly vanished.

The truth of this kiss would be our secret from now on and whatever happened in my life, I would know that I once kissed the most beautiful girl in our school . . . and very likely the entire world. Me. Curry Pot. In this moment I was no longer the dorky, overweight Indian kid who doubled as Mark Delancy's punching bag. Judy had led me into an inner sanctum where all great lovers lived. I was Elvis, I was Travolta, I was Starsky and Hutch (hey . . . it was the 70's!). It felt like I was in the last scene of a great film where the credits roll up the screen as the hero throws the heroine onto the back of his horse and rides off into the sunset never to return.

Things would never be the same from this moment on, because no one would ever again taunt me with their name calling, or their chanting, or their Jesus, or their British bulldogs, or their stupid dares, or their bloody noses, because I had conquered them. I had, in one monumental moment, conquered them all! The most beautiful girl in our class and very likely the entire world had kissed me once down in a cellar inside a beat-up stained mattress with seventeen children and Mark Delancy on top of us. I had become the king. I had become the Curry Pot Cowboy.

THE LEDGE

THE WIND WHIPPED THROUGH the small courtyard below me. I balanced precariously, shivering on a cold, hard cement ledge. I had never stood on a ledge like this before, this high up, and I didn't know how long I would be standing on it. It was getting very late, almost midnight. At six A.M. the morning bell would sound, signaling that we were to wake up and make ourselves presentable for breakfast. Would I actually be expected to stay out here for six more hours? Surely they wouldn't leave me out here all night? Someone would have to remember that I was locked outside the fourth floor Southern House dormitory window on this unfriendly ledge.

Not that breakfast was such a highlight. Undoubtedly I would once again eat dry cereal, because the two prefects at the head of the table would satisfy themselves with almost the entire contents of a single milk jug before handing it down to the third-form students like myself at the other end. The prefects were part of an elite group of sixth-form boys specifically selected by the faculty because of their superior scholastic or athletic achievements. They were in charge of the rest of the student body any time before and after the actual school day and they ran the school like storm troopers with relative impunity. If you ever complained about them or crossed them, it could mean an invitation to Toad Hall, the sixth-form recreational room behind the commissary where busted lips and kicks to the groin were the least of what you could expect.

In the six months I had been living at Woodhouse Grove Boarding School, I had seen many of my classmates limping or crying as they walked back to their dorms. I, so far, had never experienced this treatment and I intended to keep it that way. So dry cornflakes it was every morning. I had convinced myself it was just like eating a delicious bowl of salt-free crisps. In a pinch there was always water to soggy it up. Although, having tried that one morning, I realized there is nothing more depressing than eating mushy flakes out of a tasteless puddle.

After breakfast was chemistry. It wouldn't be so bad to be forgotten out here, I thought, if it meant skipping Mr. Shorey (a.k.a. Smurf)'s chemistry class. He was a fat gnome who waddled around the room and mumbled into his beard. But it was far from comfortable out on the ledge. As far as punishments doled out by the dormitory prefects went (and there were many to choose from), being locked out on a ledge four stories high in the middle of winter in nothing more than my pajamas was the most imaginative and frightening one yet. I may not have been invited to Toad Hall, but I'd already had plenty of run-ins with the prefects who made it their duty to lord their power over the younger boys. For example, there was my first run-in, a few days after I had arrived, when I was forced to hand-wash a prefect's sweaty jock strap and mud-stained rugby kit because I kept grinning at him. He seemed to be friendly and cordial and I was seeking companionship, but clearly that was not how the hierarchical system worked here and he wanted me to know it.

Then there was the time my friends Cocker, Rob, Mizzy, and I all had to stand facing a wall while one of the prefects pummeled us with a cricket ball for being late for "prep" (the two hours before bedtime when we returned to our classrooms to do our homework). We were not allowed to scream or act like it hurt; however, the giant stains of urine that spread down our legs were a clear giveaway.

Another time during prep, the same prefect had invented a far more creative punishment when he asked me to write down as many insults as I could in fifteen seconds, after which he added the words "I am a" to each one and escorted me to every classroom where I was instructed to recite them to uproarious laughter. I am a cocksucker, a motherfucker, a sisterfucker, a faggot, a Paki, a curry-breather, a shit stain, a cum stain, a hairy ballsack, a dothead, a sand nigger, a normal nigger, a piss head, an ass licker, a cunt, a bleeding cunt, a giant bucket of puss juice, a shit pisser, a spit licker, a snot guzzler, a eunuch jelly, and a puke stocking. The last two I stole from the movie *A Clockwork Orange* and William Shakespeare, respectively.

And the ledge was far more terrifying, although slightly less imaginative, perhaps, than the time I had to pick a playing card from a deck to decide how many lashes I would receive from a broken television antenna for having been caught saying my Muslim prayers after lights-out. This was a classic punishment that many of the boys received for various infractions, but praying "Paki mumbo-jumbo to Allah Walla Ding Dong," meant that the number of lashes would be doubled. I picked a jack of hearts, so ten lashes became twenty and I lost count after a dozen even though the welts on my behind continued to remind me for a few days following.

Though there were some punishments worse than the ledge, now that I thought about it. I would have stood out on a ledge in the cold for a month if it meant avoiding what I heard had happened to one of the fourth-form boys in the Atkinson House dormitory. Rumor was that he had been caught masturbating in the bathroom and, to humiliate him, he was stripped naked and forced to parade around the dormitory with his erection on full display while the other boys laughed and jeered and pummeled him with pillows and books. Sitting on a ledge till morning was perfectly fine compared to that.

As the night deepened around me, I took in my surroundings. Snow blanketed the ground below and the dark gothic stone buildings of the school, built during Queen Victoria's reign, were silhouetted perfectly against the navy blue sky like the cover of a cheap horror novel. The moon was a perfectly tilted crescent playing a casual game of peekaboo as she floated in and out of view behind the clouds.

I was glad to see the moon again. She had been a constant source of comfort for me over the last six months since my father had hugged me in the school parking lot and said, "Don't worry, soon you will make lots of great friends, beta," and my mother had tearfully kissed me, reminding me to say my nightly prayers. A few nights after that during prep, my homesickness merged with claustrophobia as I stared at the pale concrete walls of my classroom. I felt my chest tighten as tears began to rise up into my throat. Terrified they would seep out of my eyes and be seen by the other boys, I stared up at the moon and tried to breathe. As I stared I was reassured by the thought that if I could see the moon, so could my mother, and perhaps the moon could relay messages back and forth. The panic attack subsided.

However, the moon seemed silent tonight, offering no advice. Ever-present as I stood on the ledge, like a mother teaching her child independence, she floated in the cold night sky, just watching. I stared at her in return, closely examining her pockmarked face to keep myself from falling into fear and anxiety or worse still, sleep.

The window was locked from the inside. I pushed on it, a little too hard perhaps, and almost lost my balance. My foot slipped as I clutched onto the window handle with all my might. I knew someone would have to let me back in eventually. I just didn't know how long that would be.

All of this had happened because Rob's parents had sent him food, which he had decided to share with me, since our beds were next to each other.

There were two things that would keep us up after lights-out, risking the wrath of the prefects: food and naked lady pictures. I'm not sure this ever changes in a man's life, but it's particularly enticing when you are thirteen. If someone's mother had sent him food, we would risk our very lives when the prefects weren't looking by running from bed to bed passing baked goods and pastries back and forth like skilled drug runners. If someone's older brother had sent him a back issue of *Penthouse* or *Hustler*, however, there was no group sharing. We would wait all night for the images of breasts and pubic hair to be passed to us after each boy had spent an adequate amount of time with it. Since everything in school was dictated by the law of the jungle, those like me at the bottom of the food chain always went without. As it was with the cereal milk, it also was with the naked lady pictures, and I spent many nights fantasizing about both.

Rob and I were whispering about whether the chocolate or the lemon cake was better when Rob saw the creeping shadow of a prefect in the doorway behind me. In an instant, Rob vanished, as he and the cake tins were swallowed under white sheets, leaving me in mid-discussion with my torso leaning out of bed and my hands and mouth covered in cake crumbs.

Smithy shone his flashlight in my face.

"Get out of bed," he ordered.

No sooner did I stand up than I felt a fast fist to my abdomen that made me double over with pain.

"I've told you about talking after lights out, Mandi-wala," he said, pulling me up by my pajama collar. He walked over to the window and opened it. "You want to talk? Talk out here."

"What do you mean, Smithy?" I asked, facing the open sky and billowing curtains.

"Get out there!" he hissed, and shoved me out the window.

The next thing I knew I was on the ledge with the window locked behind me, convinced that this prank could only last for a few minutes before I would surely have to be let back in. However, it had been almost half an hour and no one had come to rescue me.

It was a fraction warmer now that the wind was gone. The moon had disappeared behind a giant blanket of clouds and the air was still and silent. Something else had changed and it took a moment for me to realize what it was. Until now I had been kept hopeful by the signs of life inside. I could sense the general tossing and turning, the whispering of my dorm mates, the flashlights, and occasional laughter of the prefects. But now the lights were out. The sounds had ceased. Every last person, it seemed, had gone to sleep. I was alone.

My heart began to pound as I felt the bony hand of panic around my throat. I yelled and banged on the window to be let back in, tightly holding the handle to keep my balance. A flashlight came on and a shadow from inside filled the frosted glass windowpane. I felt a huge sense of relief. Smithy must have heard the house master coming down the hallway and needed to get me off the ledge and in bed before he entered the dorm to do a headcount. To my dismay, however, he did not turn the lock on the window. Instead he shone his flashlight full in my face again, blinding me. His words came through the glass low and slow.

"Shut. Your. Fucking. Mouth," he said, then disappeared.

I turned around to face the night. All I could hear was my breathing. It grew louder and shallower as I confronted the terrifying reality that I might be left out here all night. No one could save me from this, not my parents, not the teachers, not the other boys, no one.

I managed to sit down on the cold, slightly damp ledge and was able to balance by resting my feet on a pair of bricks jutting out just below me. I peered down between my feet. The ground seemed to rush up at me as I leaned forward. I jerked back with my breath caught in my throat. I needed to secure myself, somehow, but the only thing I could do was get as much of my hand as I could wedged into the space between the handle and the window frame and hold on for support. I leaned forward again. The ground didn't seem quite as far away as it had a moment before. There was a large mound of snow that the plows had pushed directly beneath the ledge where I perched. I had begun to shiver. My fingers felt like ice on the cold metal handle and the tips of my ears burned from the frigid night air. I had to get down. There was no way I could last out here until morning. I would either freeze or fall asleep and either one meant I'd likely slip from the ledge. Why not jump and at least control my landing as much as possible?

I thought about it for some time, wondering if the giant mound of snow was enough to cushion my fall. Perhaps it was an illusion and the snow was simply blanketing an old wheelbarrow or a stack of milk crates left there by the gardener or the kitchen staff. There was no way for me to know. I needed to get a closer look. I shifted some of my weight to my feet and leaned out further from the ledge. My foot slipped on the brick and I scrambled back, holding on to the metal handle as tightly as I could. It was clearly too dangerous. I had to get down! But I was too scared. Shivering again, I huddled as far back toward the window as I could get. I squeezed my eyes shut and began to cry. I was tired and it was late but I had to keep my mind occupied and so I did the only thing I could think to do: I began to say my prayers.

I opened my mouth, but instead of Koranic verses, I heard a very different sound—laughter. Why was I laughing? I was deadly afraid and I was laughing? The prefects would hear me laughing and I would be beaten for sure, I thought.

"Stop laughing!" I told myself sternly. "Have you lost your mind?"

But the laughter continued, and as it got louder and louder, bouncing off the stone buildings and reverberating through the courtyard below, I realized it was not my laughter at all. Someone else was out here.

I looked down into the courtyard to identify the culprit, but all was still in the darkness below. I looked up toward the rooftops of the other buildings to see if one of the prefects had decided to step out onto another ledge to taunt me all night long. Finally I spotted him: a man sitting on a ledge just like mine two windows over. But this man was no prefect. This was an older man, sitting with his right leg dangling down toward the courtyard and his arms resting on his left knee as he sipped from a canteen of some sort. As I looked closer, I could make out that he was dressed in a costume, like that of a knight or a medieval king. A large red cross adorned the front of his tunic and a dark cloak fell over one shoulder. With long stringy hair and a beard, he resembled a drunken actor who, while in the middle of a play, had perhaps grown tired of his part and just decided to wander off. Either that or he was a cat burglar wearing the most impractical disguise ever made. Regardless of who he was, I was not frightened to see him. On the contrary, I was overjoyed, because, if an old drunk wearing a cape could climb up to the fourth floor, then there must be a way for a very sober thirteen-year-old in his pajamas to climb down.

"Hello," I called. "Hello!"

As I looked closer, I realized that the stranger did not need to be made aware of my presence. He already was. In fact he was staring right at me and laughing! He raised his canteen to me and took another slug, laughing uproariously as if he were toasting me across the table at a medieval feast. For the first time since I'd been pushed through the window, I forgot my fear. I was furious. Of all the people who could rescue me, what were the odds that it would be either a drunk or a fool?

"Excuse me," I shouted, trying to remain civil. "I'm glad you find this so amusing, but would you mind helping me get off this ledge? You would think that seeing a cold scared child out here in his pajamas would be somewhat alarming to you, so could you stop laughing at me, sober up for a moment, and actually do something?"

To my surprise, my speech seemed to have an effect. The stranger stopped laughing, gathered up his cape, put away his canteen, stood up and stretched. Then he looked down into the darkness below and stepped toward the edge.

"Umm . . . be careful," I called. He was behaving far too cavalierly and I was annoyed that I seemed to be more worried for his safety than he was for mine.

"Look, if you are indeed a burglar, I promise I won't tell," I continued. "Mum's the word. I never met you. I won't tell the police. I won't even mention it to anyone at school, if you just help me get down."

The stranger turned to me and stared. In the next second, without any hesitation he stepped out into thin air and leapt! He fell fast, like an arrow down into the darkness of the courtyard below. I gasped and felt my lungs freeze with the sudden influx of ice-cold air. I could not believe what had just happened. He had jumped! He'd actually jumped! I'd hoped he would save me and instead he had killed himself. I had just witnessed the suicide of a drunken, mad, medieval knight-type person.

"Fuck these fucking people," I shouted to the moon, to the empty night and the silent dorms. "Fuck that fucking fuck-head Smithy who thought leaving me out here to die was funny. Fuck that guy for jumping like that right in front of me. Fuck this fucking school, fuck the teachers, fuck my parents, fuck the moon, and fuck you, God!"

In the next moment I almost jumped out of my skin as the mad costumed stranger appeared in front of me again. He flew up from the courtyard atop a galloping horse that lifted him effortlessly through the air. He came thundering toward me. His laughter was now a bloodcurdling scream, as the horse's hooves pounded the air and its nostrils flared.

"Die, infidel!" he screamed as he swung what I initially thought was a sword, but upon closer inspection I realized was a very long television antenna.

I ducked not a moment too soon, still clinging tight to the window handle. The antenna came at me again from the other direction and this time it did the trick. I tried to avoid the blow, but it sliced me across my backside and I lost my grip. My hand slipped from the window latch, my knees buckled, and both feet slipped off their perch as I hurtled toward the darkness below, the wind whipping though my hair and ears.

Suddenly, and much sooner than I thought possible, I landed hard, splayed out on a rock—a warm, cushiony, satiny rock that seemed to have muscles and breath within it. The minute I landed on it, the rock lunged back. I heard a powerful whinny as the creature jumped, caught the wind under its belly, and leapt up out of the darkness like a full-speed locomotive. I gripped the reins of what I could now see was a beautiful white stallion! As we rose above the buildings, for a moment I could see all the way to the snow-covered rugby fields and the moonlit steeple of the chapel where we attended Sunday services.

The next moment we landed full gallop on the rooftop of Southern House dormitory. My head felt strangely heavy as I looked around wondering what on earth was happening. I put my hand to my hair and realized that it was covered in an intricately arranged turban. A coat of fine chainmail covered my neck and torso beneath a brightly colored robe. I reached up to my face and found myself caressing a long, thin black beard.

I looked up and saw that the strange knight was again galloping toward me with his trusty TV antenna raised high above his helmet.

"Come and get one in the yarbles, if ya have any yarble, ya eunuch jelly thou," he screamed.

As he got closer, I could see his face more clearly. Even though it was dirty and hairy and his hair was long and unkempt, there was no denying the voice, the eyes, the laugh. It was Smithy.

Instead of being afraid, however, I was overcome with exhilaration and adrenaline. I grabbed at my belt—this costume had to come with a sword! As I reached down into the folds of cloth, my hand fell into a satchel hanging from the horse saddle underneath me. Inside was an object I was all too familiar with. I smiled as I ran my hand across its round circumference. I held a cricket ball, hard and smooth, with stitches that pressed into my palm. The saddlebag was full of them.

I pulled one out and threw it as hard as I could at Smithy's head. He ducked as it flew past him, but I had another and another and another. I threw back my arm and sent them hurling at him at lightning speed. Some hit their target and others did not. Pretty good, I thought, since I had never been very good at cricket. As Smithy and I charged toward each other it didn't seem to matter how many balls I threw, for more knights appeared behind him, dressed identically, one after the other as if my audacity to fight back was the very thing that gave them life. Above their heads they carried large billowing banners. At first they looked like Woodhouse Grove school banners, with the green and red colors of our school shield, but as they got closer it was clear they were in fact giant pairs of dirty underwear, jock straps, and rugby kits.

Below the banners were the faces of the soldiers. I recognized them all; they were the prefects. I could hear a chant rising among their ranks, a monotone, soulless, football hooligan type–chant that I had heard many times before. I had heard it all my life, as long as I could remember.

"Let's go Paki bashing, let's go Paki bashing, let's go Paki bashing . . ."

Those words sent a chill down my spine, taking me back to a bus stop. A locker room. A playground. An alley behind my house. I instinctively began to run away. I longed to return to my cold hard ledge, now a seeming bastion of safety. I wondered what had become of me, if I had fallen and died, or fallen asleep and was suffering from hypothermia. Was I lying at the bottom of the dark courtyard in a wheelbarrow with a broken collarbone? What state would I find myself in if I ever returned?

I had to wake myself up, so I decided I would begin to sing, loudly and triumphantly, creating so much sound that I was sure to awaken.

The only song that I could think of, strangely, was the classically heroic, chest-expanding, high-flying, symphonic theme to the 1978 movie *Superman*.

This was doubly strange since I had no idea that I even remembered the theme. I had only seen the movie once. But as the knights barreled toward me, their horses galloping and the chant of "Let's go Paki bashing" getting louder and louder, I sang out the theme as defiantly as I could: dum da da dum dum da da dum, and when I got the bit where the music crescendos and Superman begins to fly, dum da daa da dum da da daa! I charged into the fray.

The knights leapt through the air and landed on all sides of me. As they did, they turned into giant snarling dogs, with gnashing teeth and saliva dripping from their mouths. I had tried to defeat them but they were far too powerful. As they closed in toward me the chant became guttural and even more terrifying, slow and low like Smithy at the window. "Kill the Paki, kill the nigger. Allah walla ding dong! Allah walla ding dong!"

Surrounded and alone, I did the only thing I could do. I looked up at the moon. I wanted to scream to her for not saving me, for leaving me here to die. But what came out of my lungs was primitive. It came from the deepest depths of my fear and confusion.

"Moooon," I cried. "Moooon!"

The snarling dogs stopped and tilted their heads skyward, and as if they had done it a thousand times before, they began to howl. Howling at the moon. The more we howled, the brighter the moon became as she hurtled across the clear night sky. The more we called out her name, the more I saw that the dogs lost their ferocity and their fangs and slowly returned to their true shape. They were schoolboys with neatly pressed hair and smartly polished shoes, in blazers and ties, standing alone and together under a vast cold sky. We were all the same under the moonlight: just a bunch of abandoned children in a world where only the strongest and most vicious survived, with no idea how to return home.

We all hunkered down as the wind grew stronger and began to envelop us. The cold night air wrapped around us and soon became white cotton sheets and rough blankets of wool. I awoke to find myself being tucked into my dorm room bed. As I looked up the window was open, and the cold winter air blew the curtains inward. The prefect turned to me as he shut the window behind him. I didn't know his name, but I had seen him around.

"Go to sleep," he said. "And don't you ever tell Smithy that I let you back in."

"I won't. Thanks," I whispered.

"Are you okay?" he asked.

"Yeah," I said, surprised at his concern. "I'm frozen stiff but I'm okay."

"Well, you're not the first to spend some time out on the ledge," he said. "It's no fun. I was out on the ledge once, so was Smithy. Behave yourself and you won't be out there again."

Then he turned and silently walked back to his bed.

My fingers, toes, and ears felt brittle and cold against the pillow. As I lay my head down to go to sleep, I knew that tomorrow would be another day not unlike yesterday and no different than the next. I closed my eyes, still hearing the sound of young schoolboys howling at the moon, and for the first time I took comfort in the strange sad awareness that perhaps I was not entirely alone.

INTERNATIONAL HOUSE OF PATEL

My father moved our family to the United States because of a word. A single word that he had first overheard in conversations among returning ex-pats and in American films. It was a word whose meaning fascinated him. A word that for my father embodied the greatest part of the greatest country in the world, and by its very definition challenged other nations to do better, to expect more from themselves, to reach for the unreachable. It was a singularly American word, a "fat" word, a word that could only be spoken with decadent pride.

That word was . . . brunch!

A stack of pancakes eight inches high with five kinds of syrup: maple, caramel, chocolate, honey, and strawberry. Eggs any style. Biscuits lathered in whipped butter. Muffins, hash browns, and as much coffee as you could drink. Orange, grapefruit, and tomato juice. French toast and a side of extra crispy *turkey* bacon and/or sausage (because, after all, we were Muslims). All for a measly $7.95.

Brunch au Akbar!

"The beauty of America," my father would say, "is that they have so much food, that between breakfast and lunch they have to stop and eat again. Breakfast and lunch! Put them together and you get brunch! Genius, right? Bloody Americans! I love them. Their English is atrocious, but they have a word for everything."

In 1982, on the advice of a transatlantic real estate agent who was selling homes and businesses to adventurous Brits wanting to emigrate to the States, my father had gone on a reconnaissance mission to see if Florida inspired him enough to sell everything we owned, leave the north of England forever, and start all over again. I was sixteen and had been sold on the idea from the moment my parents first mentioned it. Compared to my stuffy all-boys private school, and my upcoming O-level exams (that I was certain would be the beginning of my academic demise within the British public school system), moving from Bradford to Florida felt akin to the day my parents finally threw out our old black-and-white TV and replaced it with color. I was willing to leave everything in my world behind—my friends, my school, and even my brand-new clock radio—to spend one day in what I imagined would be a sun-drenched beach paradise. Just as in the Hollywood movies I had grown up with, my life would be underscored by the gentle harmonies of surf rock, my girlfriend would look like Miss Teen USA, and my best friend would be a dolphin. I couldn't wait to leave.

I remember the call he made from West Palm Beach, his excited voice on the other end of the line as he spoke to my mother, my sister, and me as we crowded around the receiver of a single rotary telephone back in Bradford.

"How is it?" my mother asked him, perhaps hoping that we could back out of this idea to once again move to a foreign land.

My parents had done this before, fifteen years earlier, leaving the steamy, spicy, colorful, shit-filled, chaotic, and familial comfort of Bombay to seek a better life halfway across the world. That time we had ended up in a snow-covered coal mining town that belched gray fumes into the gray skies of the north of England. My father, educated as a color chemist back in India, became the proprietor and sole employee of a small newspaper shop. With a portable heater below the counter warming his frozen feet during the chilly English summers, he sold cigarettes and pornography to racist gray-haired Brits who had defeated the Germans and once ruled an empire, but were now forced to watch their glorious nation be over taken by Gunga Din himself.

"It's wonderful!" he replied. His voice was almost at the top of his register with excitement. "I just ate my first American brunch and it was delicious! The only thing I don't like is that you can't get a bloody cup of hot tea in this country. They drink cold tea. Iced tea! They actually put ice in their tea! Can you imagine? They also put ice cream in Coca-Cola! Bloody Americans! I love them. Their palate is atrocious, but there seems to be nothing they won't eat."

We all laughed, enjoying his exuberance, until my mother began to cry.

A year later we were living in Florida. We had settled in Tampa since my father, while on his reconnaissance mission, had reconnected with an old college roommate who swayed him away from West Palm Beach and convinced him that Tampa was the next great American city. Consequently, my American adventure began not on the beach, but in the suburbs.

That first summer my grandparents came from India and visited us in this land of cold tea and Coke floats. Since we were now Americans who had relatives visiting, we decided it was time to partake in the American tradition of the family road trip. We piled into a rented station wagon and headed north to see the White House and the Empire State Building.

Before we left my father had gathered us together in the living room and handed us each a white T-shirt. I unfurled mine and saw that it sported an authentic and impressive IHOP logo under which were written the words “International House of *Patel*.”

“But our name isn’t Patel, Dad,” I pointed out.

“Mandviwala was too expensive,” he said. “They charge by the letter. And besides, Americans don’t know the difference.”

He did make a fair point. The specifics weren’t important. What mattered to my father was that the corn-fed American IHOP manager would be so taken with these T-shirts that we would be ensured a discount if not for our brand loyalty, then hopefully for our sheer inventiveness.

We spent the next four days sitting in a cramped station wagon and sleeping in cheap motels. Whenever we got hungry, my father would make us wait, passing sign after sign for McDonald’s and Cracker Barrel until he saw what he was looking for: the steep peacock blue rooftop that signaled his brunchtime beacon. He would excitedly pull off the freeway, open the trunk, and hand us our costumes. My sister, my mother, my Indian grandparents, and I would stand dressing and undressing in the parking lot of yet another IHOP franchise in Georgia, or South Carolina, or Maryland.

My grandmother was the most uncomfortable with this ritual because the poor woman had to pull the shirt on over her salwar kameez, transforming her left shoulder into a giant mound consisting of a delicately hand-beaded chiffon dupatta stuffed under a one-size-fits-all Gap T-shirt. She looked like she had a goiter.

Once we had all donned our costumes, we would make our way across the parking lot and sheepishly enter the franchise. It wasn't enough that this absurd spectacle was already eliciting quizzical looks and snickers from both patrons and staff, but my father had to draw further attention to it by pointing to each one of us expectantly as soon as the waitress approached our table.

"One, two, three, four, five, six," he would say, pointing to us as we tried to hide behind our oversized IHOP menus. "Funny, right?"

He would smile and stare at the young waitress until she was finally forced to fake a laugh or look away.

If there were other Indians or Pakistanis in one of the restaurants (and there always were), they would be aghast, horrified at the sheer brazenness of our extreme frugality. They would stare in open disbelief that a man could be so insensitive as to force his wife's aging Muslim parents to pass themselves off as Hindu so he could get free pancakes. Though some also likely wished that they had thought of the scheme themselves.

Our waitress was usually either a teenage girl or an older matronly-looking woman, wearing a real IHOP uniform, who would respond to our costumes with either a half-hearted smile, or overtly fake enthusiasm designed to garner a bigger tip.

"Oh that's cute, did you make those?" or "Oh my goodness, that is funny. What's a P-A-T-E-L?" or even, "Oh, wow. I didn't know you had IHOPs in Patel. Is that where y'all are from?"

The volume of these comments was usually several octaves higher than normal. It was a pitch reserved for the hearing-impaired, the immigrant, or the obvious freeloader, of which my father may have been all three.

Then, without flinching, without embarrassment, without a hint of self-awareness or restraint or propriety, my father would invariably point to me. ME! Sixteen years old, pimple-faced, hair styled in a South-Asian Afro, a person who had no hope of having sex for at least another eight years.

"My son made them in school," he would say. "For his grandmother . . . because as you can see, she has a deadly goiter."

After the third or fourth time I watched this scenario play out and the poor waitress get the not-so-subtle hint to ask the manager to see if they actually offered discounts to people wearing homemade IHOP T-shirts accompanied by dying birthday grandmothers with fake goiters, I couldn't take it anymore.

"Dad! Please!" I hissed at him across the table. "This is seriously embarrassing!"

"Embarrassing! Embarrassing?" he barked back. "This is not bloody embarrassing. You don't know embarrassing."

"Whatever," I mumbled.

"Let me tell you what is really embarrassing," he continued. "Having only one pair of shoes, that's embarrassing. Having to study for your exams under a street lamp because you don't have your own room, that's embarrassing. Hanging off the side of a train on your way to work because it's so crowded and you can't afford a seat, that's embarrassing."

I could see the waitress returning from the back of the restaurant, a bemused look on her face. I really didn't want to be there when she got to the table and explained that just this once IHOP could give my father a 10 percent discount on the meal, or whatever other paltry salve she had been authorized to apply to this overly enthusiastic customer.

"I'm not hungry, anyway," I said and slipped out of the booth. This was a lie; I was starving. But before my father could grab my arm or catch my eye I was out the door. I decided I'd rather sit in the car during every meal than wear his stupid T-shirt ever again. For the rest of the trip my mother was forced to bring me takeout containers of lukewarm pancakes, eggs, and hash browns already growing soggy in a puddle of melted butter and syrup.

In truth, I understood my dad more than I was letting on. I knew that to my dad, America was Willy Wonka's chocolate factory and he was a ten-year-old who had won a golden ticket. I remembered when we first arrived in Florida, my father and I would go to the grocery store produce section carrying a camera, where he would pose next to giant cantaloupes and engorged honeydews. He took smiling pictures of his family surrounded by gastronomical excesses: giant bottles of cherry Coke, humongous jars of peanut butter, and industrial-sized cereal boxes that could feed an Indian family of ten. He would then send these photographs back to my aunt in India, who for many years afterward believed that Albertson's and Safeway weren't mere food stores but fantastical American theme parks.

Whenever there was an offer to buy one and get the other for half price, my father was the first in line. His ability to consume knew no bounds and there was not a promotion or an advertisement that did not interest him. He embraced America and its consumer culture with open arms and an even wider mouth.

While my father loved excess, I dreaded his impromptu gastronomical field trips. Even before the IHOP debacle, I distinctly remember a fight we had at our local Baskin Robbins. His favorite flavor was something like Chocolate Pecan Fudge Butter Nutter with extra sprinkles and M&M's. When I ordered plain old chocolate he took it as an insult.

"They have thirty-two flavors, thirty-two bloody flavors," he said, "and you order chocolate? Chocolate you can get anywhere in the world. Why did we come to America? It is an insult to every beggar on the streets of India to simply order chocolate. We didn't sacrifice everything and come to the land of plenty so that you could be satisfied with bloody plain old chocolate ice cream. Now order like an American. Two scoops, different flavors, extra toppings on a sugar cone."

Things got even worse a few weeks after our road trip when my father decided to break the tense silence that had festered between us by insisting that I accompany him to get pizza. After ordering two large pies (because the second was half-price), he asked me what I wanted to drink.

"I just want a medium soda," I said.

"Get the large," he said.

"I don't want it."

"You get the Extra Large Gulp for only thirty-nine cents more."

"No, I just want the medium."

"It is only thirty-nine cents more and you get twice as much. We will take the large one."

"I don't want it."

"Damn it, son!" he yelled.

His voice was starting to attract the attention of the other customers in line. I could feel the back of my neck getting flushed with embarrassment.

"When will you become an American?" he continued. "Okay, pour the extra thirty-nine cents-worth into a cup and I will drink it later."

I turned on him, furious. "See? You're doing it again. You just can't help yourself, can you?"

"What happened? What did I do? It's only thirty-nine cents more," he said. "What is wrong with you?"

"What's wrong with *me*?" I laughed. "What is wrong with you? When will *you* become an American? An American who lives in the land of plenty but knows how to practice a little moderation and restraint. Someone who doesn't have so little dignity that they are willing to siphon off a half-liter of soda just to take advantage of a stupid thirty-nine cents saving?"

My father looked at me without saying a word. His face was expressionless for a moment and then slowly he began to smile.

"You think Americans practice moderation and restraint?" he asked.

"Umm . . . yeah," I nodded, knowing I might have made a strategic error in saying so.

"Are you a bloody idiot?" he asked, his usually high-pitched voice now dropping an octave, giving gravitas to what he was about to tell me.

"Son, this is a country where you can walk into a grocery store and purchase a 'turducken.' Have you ever heard of a turducken?"

I shook my head.

"A turducken is a turkey that is stuffed with a duck that is stuffed with a chicken that is stuffed with a sausage. No one except an American would think of eating such a thing. I have never sent a picture of one to your aunt because I am afraid if she knows something like that exists, she will kill herself. Do you get my point?"

His face was deadly serious. I did get it.

"And as far as dignity goes," he continued, "no one had more dignity than your grandfather, a man who woke up every day and could only afford chai and bread for breakfast, and yet he dressed in a clean starched white shirt and held on to his briefcase and stood with dignity as he hung on to the side of a train on his way to work."

I stared at the ground for a moment collecting my thoughts. I had been schooled.

Then he put his hand on the back of my shoulder.

"How about we forget the pizza? Instead, in your grandfather's name, let's go eat a ridiculously large brunch."

Part II

WELCOME HOME: THE TRAIN

"BANG! YOU'RE DEAD!"

The source of this sudden assault was a boy with olive skin, perfect white teeth, and big brown eyes. He lifted his pistol and fired at me with the plastic toy.

"Bang! You're dead!" he yelled out again. "Bang! Bang! Bang!"

He kept firing, creating a level of imaginary carnage that rivaled the bloodiest video game. He was about seven years old and his banging had disrupted the peace and quiet of every passenger in the railroad car. Most were business men on their way home from meetings at their head offices in London, attempting to read or work as they passed away the two hours and change that it took British Rail to get from London's King Cross Station to the North of England.

I was among the weary few trying to sleep, still fighting the jet lag that always felt like it lasted two or three months for me when I travel eastwards across the Atlantic. The last thing I needed was to be yelled at by some doe-eyed, dimpled assassin who was both an incredibly cute little bastard and . . . a little bastard. I played dead and closed my eyes as soon as the shooting started, hoping he would realize he couldn't kill me any more than he already had and let me rest in peace. No such luck.

The ineffective maternal reprobate responsible for this little devil was a beautiful young Muslim woman. At least her face was beautiful, for she was otherwise covered in a hijab from head to toe. I had seen her and her son earlier on the platform while we waited for the train. Our eyes had met for a brief moment and I had smiled and stepped closer to make a comment about the weather, or train travel, or anything, but it was not to be. As soon as our eyes met she had immediately looked down and away. Humility? Pride perhaps? Or perhaps it was just the natural reaction of a woman, especially a Muslim woman. Looking a strange man in the eyes might be unseemly or even dangerous. Perhaps she was warding off my overly friendly American demeanor that is so often discomforting to Europeans. I couldn't tell. I knew nothing about her, but she was familiar, a part of a world I had left behind when we moved to America.

She was a grown up version of the daughters of the Pakistani shopkeepers from whom we would buy candy when I was a boy. I recalled the way they would stare at us from their upstairs bedroom windows, watching us play football or cricket on the street below, unable to come down and join the game. Like them, she now sat a few feet away in the seats facing mine, close enough so that our feet might have brushed against each other, and stared out the window at a world passing by. She seemed deep in thought or worry as she stared at the English countryside, or perhaps she was just trying to enjoy a few moments of bliss while her son was otherwise engaged. After a moment, instead of demanding peace and quiet from her rowdy son, she suggested that he not only continue his rampage, but now do it while sporting a brand new cowboy hat, that she had no doubt purchased from some cheap street vendor in Piccadilly Circus.

Our eyes connected again for a moment as she turned to watch her son. As large and open as they were, they also kept something hidden. She held my gaze for a moment and looked me up and down. I was about to smile, to say something humorous, something that might make her laugh, but in the next moment she looked away again. Damn, she was beautiful. Flawless, like a painting. The fact that I couldn't stop staring at her, and she knew I couldn't stop staring at her, was making me well . . . it was pissing me off.

She was young, probably in her late twenties. Too young to have a child that old, I thought.

"Put on your cowboy hat, Ali love," she said as she handed her son the hat. Her West Yorkshire accent gave away that not only were we both from immigrant Muslim families, we grew up in the same region. I might have still sounded like her had my parents not taken me to America as a teenager where, perhaps due to my penchant toward mimicry, I lost most of my Yorkshire brogue for a distinctly American drawl after just a few short years.

It seemed to me our similarities were limited, however. Though we came from the same part of the world and the same religion, I had risen above the parochial upbringing I felt I had been born into. I prided myself on being an artist and had seen the world. I stared at her now as one would stare at a recreation of a different hominid species in a display at the National History Museum, knowing that there is some root gene that connects both of you, but recognizing that you took very different paths in your evolutionary history.

In the last two decades I had become disillusioned with my relationship to Islam–in truth I had seen the inside of more bars than mosques. I mostly defined prayer as an excuse to ask God for things:

"Please, please, please, Allah, let me get this part. I promise I will give to the poor," I would say after an audition. "I will pray five times a day if you just make it so they cast me as Islamic terrorist number 3."

Or whenever I was afraid: "Please, Allah, let that just have been turbulence and not the explosion of an engine," I would say as I clenched the armrest of my airplane seat.

"Please, Allah, let this HIV test be negative," I would say after a night of poor decision making and drunken sex. "I promise I will give to the poor and marry a nice Muslim girl and always use a condom from now on."

I treated the creator of the Universe as my very own personal spiritual Santa Claus, showering me with good fortune if I was a good boy. It felt selfish and dirty and I wanted it to be different but I didn't know how. The upshot was that I couldn't live with Islam and I couldn't live without it so I mostly just ignored it.

I found myself making assumptions about the young Muslim woman, probably because I figured she was making assumptions about me. She was subjugated, I decided, un-liberated, forced by tradition or fear to dress the way she did. Though it did occur to me that I was the one who, as a younger man, had worn Islam as a costume. I remembered a gold pendant that I had worn discreetly around my neck for some time in my twenties. It said Allah in Arabic. It was a gift from some relative and in the times that it caught the attention of my caucasian and/or Judeo Christian friends, I felt like I was subtly expressing some deep truth about my dislocated identity;

a gang sign of sorts that identified with my core culture and religion. This was before Sept 11th when many Americans thought the word "Muslim" referred to a type of cloth. They tried to be respectful.

"That's beautiful," they would say. "Is that your name in Indian?"

"No, it says Allah," I would reply.

"Allah? What's that mean?"

"It's the name of God."

"Which God?" they would ask.

"The Muslim God."

Then came the comment that I hated the most:

"I didn't know you were religious."

"I'm not," I would shoot back, looking down at the pendant and realizing that even I didn't know why I wore it. Perhaps I simply wanted them to recognize the inherent contradiction I felt inside me all the time. That my seeming similarity to them and their traditions and their culture was as much a costume piece as this pendant was. The question they asked was valid. If I didn't identify with Islam, then why did I wear a pendant that said Allah around my neck? I suppose it was for the same reason I wore a baseball cap when I knew nothing about baseball.

As I watched the beautiful young mother it became clear that I was the one who struggled to reconcile my identity with the western world around me. She seemed perfectly satisfied to sit on a train and have people assume she was living in the middle ages. Perhaps that's why I was fascinated with her. She seemed comfortable with who she was and what she believed. The more I studied her the more I knew that it was me, not her, that was weak. I had been blown this way and that my entire life, wearing whatever identity I could in order to be accepted. Perhaps this was why I had chosen to become an actor. Seeking invisibility and notoriety at the same time is something actors understand. I was always jealous of those people that knew who they were. That knew what they believed and didn't care who agreed with them or not. Perhaps I was the one that would eventually die out from natural selection, not her. But having said that, she was also just really fucking annoyingly beautiful.

"BANG! BANG!"

He was at it again. He realized that he had not finished the job the first time since my eyes were open and looking in his mother's direction. This time he snuck up, peeking his tiny face and giant cowboy hat over the seat behind her. I wanted to snatch his stupid pistol and throw it down the aisle in the hope that he would go running after it, but instead I just smiled at him. She noticed me smiling and for a moment I thought I had traversed the divide that separated us. I noticed that I was not smiling at her son but at her, right at her, right at her face, right into her eyes. She did not smile back. Once again, she looked away. "Fuck you!" I thought to myself. There are no points in heaven for not smiling at someone. I stared at her reflection in the window as English trees and cottages and farms hurtled across her perfectly shaped nose, her smooth cheeks and her full lips. A small lock of dark brown hair that should have remained hidden peeked out from the edge of her hijab. That soft brush of hair was incredibly erotic. I turned away, embarrassed at my reaction, and found myself staring into another, smaller set of big brown eyes.

Since he was not going to let me sleep, I decided to engage with the little brown cowboy.

"Do you have a girlfriend?" I asked.

The young boy rolled his eyes and then burst into tiny giggles like his body was being riddled with the very same bullets he had been firing at me.

"No," he said, going beet red and answering with the kind of tone reserved for adults who ask stupid questions. "No. Duh. I'm only seven."

"Mum," he yelled, "that man asked me if I had a girlfriend!"

I was mortified. I felt her eyes shift as she continued to look out of the window. Like a lioness sitting in the grass, seemingly unaware, but completely focused on her cub, she watched my reflection for any signs of misconduct. Hearing my question out loud like that made it sound far more incriminating than was my intention. I could feel other eyes on me. The older woman sitting across the aisle looked up from her book and made note of the potential child molester on the train. The man behind me stirred ever so slightly from his nap and accidentally on purpose kicked the back of my chair as if to say, "Are you a fucking moron? You had him in the palm of your hands. You could have kept him quiet, done the parenting that his mother refuses to do and instead you ask a little boy the one question that will drive him into a hysterical fit of confusion and embarrassment. Idiot!"

"I'm an American cowboy," the boy said in his thick Northern English accent. "Like on the telly. I want to be a cowboy on the telly when I grow up, but my Mum says I can't."

"Well maybe she will change her mind," I said. She heard me. I knew that she heard me, but still she didn't meet my eyes.

"Have you ever been on the telly, mister?" he asked, grinning from ear to ear.

I stared at him. I had two paths in front of me at this moment. I could lie and deny being on television whereupon, as soon as he was bored, my conversation with this little man would come to an end. Or I could tell him the truth, that I had indeed appeared on "the telly." This would peak his interest and perhaps turn me into something of a hero, which would then no doubt capture the imagination of his mother and perhaps even make her notice me.

"Yes, I have," I replied. No sooner had the words escaped my lips than a shriek of hysterical proportions whistled through the cabin of the train like an alarm. Every passenger was jolted awake, and I had become not only the agitator of said shriek, but also an accomplice to this little boy.

Worst of all, I knew that she knew that I was attempting to flirt with her, pathetically, through her son. A woman who I clearly would have had as much success with if she had been a Hasidim or Amish. What on earth did I hope to achieve? I was a young, relatively handsome single male, who could be flirting with any number of attractive single women if I wanted to, so why? Why the hijab wearing Muslim girl with the annoying kid? It was a good question, one I had no answer for, but it was clear I wanted more than her attention. Deep down, I wanted to break her. I wanted her to want me. I fantasized about her losing control of her values, her tradition her culture, her faith; I fantasized that not only her clothes but her soul would come undone. I saw her hijab as simply a challenge to overcome on the way to discovering her hidden sexuality. I wanted to touch her breasts, her legs, her skin. I wanted to conquer her and make her mine.

The boy turned to his mother and screamed, "Mum, that man is on the telly!"

She simply pulled a handkerchief from her purse and wiped his nose.

The boy's big brown eyes locked on me again while his mother put the snot-stained tissue in her bag and pulled out a magazine, some celebrity rag that tracked the torrid goings on of the Beckhams or the Royal Family. I was surprised. In spite of appearances, we were not that different. Like me, she had grown up in the west. Like me, she was seduced by celebrity and pop culture. In the next instant, almost as if he could read my mind, the boy stepped across the aisle and planted himself next to me. He started asking questions in rapid fire.

"Are you from America, mister?"

"What's it like on the telly?"

"Are you famous?"

"Are you a movie star?"

"Are you from Hollywood?"

"Do you like my gun?"

Again, I found myself trying to catch his mother's eye, but her face was frozen, now staring into the magazine.

"New York," I said.

"And are you on the telly in New York?" he asked

"Sometimes," I said.

"My mum doesn't watch the telly," he said. "She hates the telly. She says it's full of lies."

I smiled at her and, just for a moment, she looked up and held my gaze. It was like the sun peeking out from behind a blanket of clouds, but I knew it was a signal. A recognition of the vast insurmountable divide that separated us. A divide called East and West, Tradition and Modernity, Islam and America. Or perhaps she was just letting me know that she was way out of my league and in spite of my American charm, my celebrity, my seeming playfulness with her son, I could in no way seduce her. She would never accept me because she saw my ultimate intentions as self serving, shameful, and driven by my ego. That I possessed no sacredness, no tradition, no faith. In her gaze I saw her perception of me as a soul that had drifted, seduced by a false world, like the one in the pages of her magazine. In her mind I must have seemed a child, much like her own son, raised on a diet of celebrity, violence, and processed foods, brandishing my American weapon of arrogance and superiority.

As we finally arrived at our destination, the conductor's thickly accented voice blared over the intercom, and the red brick station walls took the place of the fields and meadows of the Yorkshire countryside. She grabbed her son with one hand and luggage with the other and made her way through the crowd of passengers exiting the train. Behind her the magazine slipped from the polyester seat and landed atop her son's forgotten cowboy hat. As I rose from my seat to retrieve my luggage from the overhead bin, I turned and looked out the window to see if I could catch one final glimpse of them, but they were gone. Instead, I found myself staring at a cold blue-and-white sign that read "Welcome to Bradford."

NO LAND'S MAN: BECOMING AASEEEEF

IN 1982, MY FATHER, MY MOTHER, my sister, and I heeded Ronald Reagan's message to the world that it was morning again in America. We had very little idea what that meant, though we assumed that a morning in America would be much nicer than a dreary afternoon in the north of England, so we came. We replaced our red brick semi-detached bungalow with a chimney for a lime-green stucco house with a swimming pool. We replaced our sweaters and boots with shorts and flip-flops. We replaced the sound of magpies with the sound of tropical insects, and we came to the great state of Florida to embrace the new sunrise called the 1980s.

Soon after arriving, I found myself a junior in an all-American high school in the middle of Tampa. I quickly discovered that compared to my British boarding school, this new school was like a vacation. There was no official school uniform to speak of unless you included cut-off shorts, T-shirts, and a mullet. I also noticed that there seemed to be a casual informality between teachers and students. American public school students didn't wait to speak until they were spoken to, and teachers and students seemed to even share laughter and inside jokes, which was frankly unnerving for me, having come from a school where detention was the punishment in store for anyone who dared to speak before raising one's hand or being spoken to.

The school was clearly divided into two major groups: athletes and everyone else. The athletes wielded so much power over the goings-on at the school that occasionally actual classes would be cancelled so students could congregate at the football field to watch a pep rally for the upcoming game. Back in England I knew three students who had had been expelled for going to see a Leeds United soccer game during the school day; here it seemed this kind of behavior was mandated by the school itself. Students painted their faces and cheered and screamed for their players, while cheerleaders performed impressive acrobatics, all culminating in a kind of warrior-nation cry for blood and battle against an opposing school.

The school also had another major division: race. This divide was clearest in the lunchroom cafeteria where, with an occasional exception, white students sat with white students, black students sat with black students, Hispanics sat with Hispanics, and the two East Asian students sat with the math teacher.

I stepped into this world not knowing where to sit. Since having moved from a city with one of the largest South Asian populations in Europe to Tampa, a city that had maybe one Indian restaurant, I may as well have been the man who fell to Earth.

I realized I needed my own cafeteria clan-mate, so I tried to befriend the easiest and most familiar target: the one other Indian student in my entire high school. He was in the school band and on the baseball team, so let's just say he was quite popular. The first time I heard him speak, however, I couldn't help but be amused that he pronounced his name with a distinct southern drawl. Dilip (d'-lip) had become Dee-leap. I had never heard the Americanization of an Indian name before and even today, many years later, I find it disconcerting when I hear second-generation South Asians pronounce their own names incorrectly. The hard T of Sheetal or Namita is softened and rolls away to sound less ethnic. The clipped vowel of Deepak (dee-puk) becomes Deepaaak, Akbar (uk-bur) becomes Aaakbaaaar. I once even heard of a Pakistani kid named Aurungzeb (ar-ung-zeb) who was named after the great Moghul Emperor of the same name, but in order to avoid pronunciation mishaps, he changed his name to Orange. I don't even know how you get from Aurungzeb to Orange unless you are a seven-year-old, but nevertheless the image of an emperor who turned himself into an orange in order to be accepted has always resonated with me on a very deep level.

My first conversations with Dilip were awkward, as he always seemed to be looking past me, waiting for one of his friends to rescue him. He had a point, since other than the fact that our parents were born in the same country, we really had very little in common. He was all-American and I was mostly English, and our interactions had the distinct feeling of two brown kids forced to play together because their parents told them they had to be friends. It soon became clear that he saw me as a social liability. After a week or so he stopped acknowledging me in the hallway when he walked by with his baseball buddies. This didn't surprise me—rejection of one's own kind in favor of the dominant culture was a survival technique that I had seen before.

A few years before in England, a Sikh student had joined our school. One day out on the quad the white kids were taunting me with the word Paki, a common slur toward Indians or Pakistanis.

The Sikh boy, himself technically a Paki, was also standing within taunting distance. He watched as the English kids shoved and pushed me as I walked to class, one of them trying to trip me, another throwing a soccer ball at the back of my head. In that moment he made a strategic decision. At the time it was confusing, but in retrospect I give him credit for it. He ran over to me, grabbed me by my shirt, looked at the English kids, and then landed his fist right into the side of my face. The English schoolboys cheered as he engaged his boots and his elbows so that I fell to the ground and went fetal until the blows got weaker and the cheers grew stronger and he was eventually hoisted away as their hero. Brilliant. From that day on, unlike me, no one ever picked a fight with him or dared call him Paki.

I had even done it myself. When I was ten years old my cousin Munir came to visit us in England from Bahrain, where his family lived. I despised him. I didn't want to be associated with him or his accent. I treated the poor kid with contempt, making fun of him among my friends. I didn't know why at the time, I just didn't like him. In retrospect I realized I was jealous. Munir seemed to be okay with the person he was. He was okay with his accent, he was okay with his fashion sense, he was not trying to fit in, not trying to be accepted by anyone. He was just a kid and he didn't think much about it. It was baffling to me that he had not learned something that I had learned very early on: The world is a much easier, friendlier place when white people like you.

Munir didn't know this for two reasons. First, he was brought up in a world where everyone looked like him. Second, his family was wealthy. His father (my uncle) had made quite a fortune as a successful businessman. While my father stood behind the counter of his own store, Munir's father employed ten men like my father standing behind the counters of many stores. I admired Munir for his self-confidence, which I expressed by punching him in the mouth when I found that he had decided to borrow my five-speed British-made VMX bicycle.

So, following my failure to become friends with Dilip, I found myself without an ally or a group that I could call my own in this new American petri dish. It was only a matter of time, therefore, before I got involved with the wrong crowd: The Actors.

My mother had suggested that I take a course that hadn't been offered in my British school. She had spotted acting on a list of what American high schools call "electives." Knowing that I'd enjoyed being part of a children's theater group back in England, she suggested that I sign up. I did, and in doing so I found my true cafeteria clan-mates.

I became one of the drama kids, those histrionic thespians, comedians, tech nerds, and attention-seeking dorks, drawn to the limelight of the high school auditorium. We were all shapes and sizes and had varying degrees of talent, but drama class was not about talent, it was about celebrating our individual uniqueness amid a high school culture of conformity. We were residents of the island of misfit toys, a place where you could exchange the skin you came in for the possibility of becoming anything and anyone. The drama department did manage to put on a couple of plays each year, which we all got to participate in one way or another, but classes mostly consisted of games and improvisation exercises. It was a sanctuary of play and freedom where there was no right or wrong way to be.

Unlike the well-travelled offspring of business tycoons and diplomats back in boarding school, the drama kids I befriended were mostly middle-class American kids who hadn't met many Indian people before. And even fewer like me with a thick English accent, which is probably why during improvisations I often ended up playing either an alien or an English lord, or an alien who happened to also be an English lord. I even developed my own go-to character: a half-lizard, half-human with a funny walk that made everyone laugh and let me finally feel accepted in this foreign land. Perhaps I'd been too quick to judge poor Aurungzeb.

Truth be told, I was wholeheartedly accepted by my new drama buddies, and except for my accent and the occasional question about life in England, there was not a whole lot of conversation about my background pre-Florida. It didn't seem to matter that I was Indian or English or Muslim because like everyone else it was assumed that eventually, I would be readily absorbed into the tapestry that is Americana.

The difference between being an Indian immigrant in England and in America was that in England, despite (or perhaps due to) the long history between the two cultures, no matter what I did to be accepted, I was never considered truly British. In fact, as far I can tell, the British are mostly mistrusting of foreigners. Perhaps it's understandable, after defending their tiny island from invasion again and again for thousands of years. The irony about America is that even with all the flag waving and overt nationalism, I found the opposite to be true. Generally speaking, Americans are open, accepting, and un-cynical people who take to new things quickly and easily. The downside of this seems to be that in a country made up almost entirely of immigrants, there is little curiosity about other cultures. Perhaps because the American identity has been so tied to self-sufficiency and exceptionalism, many Americans assume that everyone would be American, if they had the choice, surely.

In other words, Americans think about the rest of the world the same way New Yorkers think about the rest of America: they don't. Which is why when I woke up one day to find that my name was no longer Aasif (aah-sif), but instead I had been given a brand new American moniker, Aaseeeef, I didn't mind at all.

NO LAND'S MAN: YOU CAN'T BE MICHAEL JACKSON ALL THE TIME

YOU CAN'T BE MICHAEL JACKSON all the time, unless you are Michael Jackson." This was the title of a poem I wrote while lying on the floor of my friend Roy's bedroom during my senior year of high school, while in a marijuana-induced haze of lucidity. It was 1984 and MTV had recently launched on American cable television. It was the first of its kind and would revolutionize the music industry as a channel dedicated solely to music videos—by white artists. That's right. It wasn't a stated purpose, per se. I don't believe it was part of their marketing campaign, but let's just say the network was suspiciously sans R&B. If one was looking for Stevie Wonder or the Gap Band, one mostly got British punk, new wave, heavy metal, and glam metal, a tragic combination of Led Zeppelin and Liberace that aliens might one day use as a justification for destroying our tiny blue planet. But all that changed with the release of one monumental album: Michael Jackson's *Thriller*.

Thriller quickly became the bestselling album in the world with people dancing to "Billie Jean" as far away as Mumbai and Tokyo, a phenomenon not seen since Elvis or the Beatles. But what was equally as amazing as Michael's meteoric rise from ordinary pop star to the King of Pop was his striking physical transformation. His nose had been pinched, his chin squared, and his eyes lifted. Eventually he no longer looked like an African-American man at all. Instead, his delicately miniaturized features looked more like those of a beautiful Indian girl.

That same year the drama department at my high school decided that instead of producing a traditional fall play, they would put on a variety show in collaboration with the music department. The drama students were asked to perform some kind of musical number, even if their lack of singing ability left them to resort to lip-synching, for which there was an actual category. This was absurd to me, since lip-synching requires no talent at all; I would rather listen to bad karaoke than watch pretty good lip-synching. Initially I decided to boycott the show entirely, but a few weeks before the performance I changed my mind . . . because of Michael Jackson.

It would be fair to say that most Indian immigrant parents would assert two important restrictions on their sons before entering high school: "No dames and no drugs." I use the word dames here simply for alliteration purposes—no Indian parent would use the word *dames*. To be fair, no non-Indian parent would use the word *dames*, unless your dad happens to be a James Cagney impersonator. My larger point is that up until my senior year I had never partaken of either. However, as my interest (and frustration) in the former increased, my attraction to the latter did as well. If only being a 125-pound geeky Indo-British theater nerd with an

Afro who specialized in funny walks had somehow made me more attractive to women, I may never have settled for drugs as my act of rebellion.

When I say drugs, I don't mean hard drugs, or even medium-soft drugs; I mean marijuana. This probably sounds innocent enough, but for someone who had never even kissed a girl or tasted wine, it might as well have been crack. Actually, it was not the pot that I was drawn to; in fact, for a long time I refused to inhale and only pretended that I was high. I just wanted to hang out with the guys who were smoking pot because they seemed cool, funny, and intellectual.

Unlike the rest of the kids in high school, Roy and Rick, my soon-to-be stoner friends, were not listening to Duran Duran or going to the mall to play video games and watch Molly Ringwald movies. They were two handsome white guys with 4.0 GPAs who had given up student government to be actively counter-culture. They didn't care what anyone thought of them as they passionately discussed for hours on end the literary merits of Jack Kerouac and Jim Morrison. I realize now this is just what happens when you are stoned, but at the time they seemed completely unlike myself and the other kids in drama. Most importantly, unlike me, Roy and Rick seemed to be having lots of sex . . . with dames.

Roy and Rick reminded me of some of the boys in my British boarding school, super-smart kids from wealthy families who would snort glue behind the cricket field. I was never foolhardy enough to join them, but I wondered what it must take to risk being suspended or even expelled. Perhaps you had to be incredibly angry, I thought, to be able to say "Fuck you" to the school, to your parents, to risk ruining your future. As an immigrant kid whose parents had sacrificed so much to give me the life I had, I never felt I had the luxury to express my anger in that way, but I was nevertheless envious of those that did.

In Roy and Rick I found a similar expression of anger and rebelliousness. They both came from wealthy, divorce-traumatized homes. Unlike at my house, where my parents had never heard of personal space and if I had a friend over my mother would walk in to my bedroom every five minutes with offerings of Indian delicacies or random food items like peaches, Roy's parents never seemed to make an appearance. We would spend hours after school and on the weekends getting stoned in Roy's basement bedroom and freaking out on the few occasions the front door slammed. We spent a lot of time driving around in Roy's beat-up sky-blue Volkswagen Bug blasting Beatles tunes and discussing Nietzsche while baked out of our minds.

On one weekend during one such car ride, a few minutes after Roy and I had picked up Rick from a local pizza restaurant where he waited tables, I experienced something that changed the rest of my high school experience. As we drove up North Dale Mabry Highway out of town, toward the open fields of north Tampa, we toked and smoked like three Easy Riders. Roy had forgotten his cassette of *The White Album* so we blasted the radio and, since it was the eighties, it was only a matter of time before the familiar drum beat and weeping falsetto of "Billie Jean" began to squeeze its way through Roy's tinny speakers. We didn't care, we sang along like it was Steppenwolf's "Born to be Wild," rolling down the windows as we let the humid Florida wind whip us into a sixty-mile-per-hour frenzy. As Roy floored the pedal we accelerated just as Michael hit the all-too-familiar chorus and I leaned forward from the backseat throwing my head out of the passenger window, screaming to the surprised shoppers in the Winn-Dixie parking lot, "She says I am the one. But the *kiiiiiiid* is not my son!"

Rick turned to me, his eyes bloodshot, his face beet-red, his surfer dude blonde locks wildly blowing like his entire head was enveloped in flames, and shouted, "Oh my God. Listen to you. You sound like Michael Jackson, dude."

He was right! And I was as surprised as he was. It seemed that without really trying I was managing to hit those high falsetto notes and doing a pretty good impersonation.

Earlier that year, Michael Jackson had sealed his stature as being bigger than Jesus while performing at the Motown twenty-fifth anniversary celebration; a single glove, a fedora, and the moonwalk all came together in a magical moment. Michael seemed to walk on water that night. Truth be told, it was not the first time I had ever seen the moonwalk—the black kids in school had been popping and breakdancing outside the lunch room for almost a year before I saw Michael do it on TV. I had even tried doing it myself in my bedroom late at night, but I always looked less like I was dancing and more like I was being riddled with bullets. I lacked three basic components: grace, control, and coordination. But while many of us had seen the moonwalk before, just the same way many had seen a magic trick before Houdini ever put on a show, no one had ever seen it elevated with the style and attitude that Michael gave it. So in that drug-induced moment in the back of Roy's sky-blue Volkswagen, I made a decision that would change the rest of my high school experience. The school variety show would have its very own Michael Jackson.

Rick's girlfriend had taped the Motown performance, and since my family didn't own a VCR, I went over to her house every night after school to watch the tape and memorize the kicks and squeals and the part where he jumps up and down and screams, "She led me to her room, hey, hey, hey." I practiced that dance everywhere, all the time. I danced in the shower, to the thumping of my mother on the other side of the bathroom door yelling, "What are you doing in there? Why are you taking a shower at two o'clock in the afternoon?"

I danced in my sister's bedroom when she was not home in order to gain inspiration and ape Michael's pained facial expressions from the posters that covered her walls.

I even broke into the dance one night before bed, while I was grabbing a glass of milk. My parents' bedroom was just off the kitchen of our small two-bedroom bungalow. With my first jump I woke my father, who emerged from bed to the sight of his teenage son kicking and twirling and emitting piercing high-pitched squeals while holding a glass of milk and wearing only his underwear at two in the morning. He must have wondered in that moment, as he watched me from the shadows, why he had ever come to this country. In the middle of a sliding moonwalk across the linoleum floor I was startled back to reality by his quiet voice saying, "I think it's time for bed."

Around the same time that my Michael Jackson transformation was in its pupa stage, my grandparents came to visit us from India. They clearly wondered what had become of their grandson. I wore dark shades, my Indo-fro was Jheri-curled, and I would spend hours in my bedroom singing and dancing with my Walkman on my head. Roy and Rick even started calling me Michael.

After much provocation from my sister I even deigned to perform for my grandparents. I couldn't imagine how this was going to go over, but at least it would explain why I kept jumping up on to my tiptoes all the time. My grandparents looked puzzled as they sat in the living room with my mom next to them. My sister hit the cassette player and as the song began I came out from my bedroom wearing shades and one sparkly glove. I began singing too early in the music so I started again. This time I attempted the 360-degree spin and my shades flew off and landed by my grandmother's feet. I don't think she knew if she was meant to laugh or not. I sang and danced through the rest of the song, missing notes and missing steps. A couple of times I even lost my balance completely and collapsed to the floor. By the end I was exhausted but had learned two very important lessons: singing and dancing at the same time is really, really hard, and moonwalking on a carpet just looks like you are trying to wipe something off the bottom of your shoe.

Despite my poor display my family was supportive. Even though my grandmother didn't understand what it all meant, my less-than-average homage to Michael Jackson brought a smile to her face. For the rest of their visit she would walk into my bedroom every day and sing "Billy Jesus not my lawyer." She had no idea what she was saying, and it didn't matter. She was now a fan.

For most of the following week, I kept practicing while feeling increasingly sick to my stomach. I realized that stoned people make impulsive decisions that lack judgment and that this was the backbone of the "Say No to Drugs" campaign. I also realized that singing like Michael and dancing like Michael at the same time was probably out of the question for a kid with asthma and so I reluctantly switched my name from the singing category to the lip-synch category, knowing full well that the only way this would work was if I nailed those turns and kicks. My moonwalk had to look like my shoes were made of glass.

The day of the variety show arrived and my transformation was complete. I was about to lip-synch "Billie Jean" for the entire student body.

I walked out in the darkness and stepped into a spotlight at center stage. My heart was pounding and in an instant my mouth seemed to lose all moisture. My limbs felt heavy as I assumed a familiar pose. The audience recognized the silhouette but not the person and there was a murmur that went through the auditorium. Before I was ready for it to happen, the familiar throbbing beat began and students began to look at each other. A whistle pierced the air and I heard an "Oh yeah!" as I reached up with my makeshift glittered glove, drenched in sweat, and slid my fingers across the brim of my fedora. Here we go, I thought, as I thrust out my hip and kicked my right leg straight and hard. A girl screamed, "I love you!" I heard another voice scream, "Hell yeah!" Then another, and another, and in an instant something felt different. For the first time I was not just recreating choreography—I was inhabiting it.

A confidence began to come over me that I had never experienced before. I felt strong and graceful as I began to release my anger, rebelliousness, sexuality, and playfulness through the pounding of Michael's rhythm. As the drumbeat gave way to the first few lyrics I turned from profile to face front. There was an explosive scream from the audience as I swallowed and opened my mouth, becoming a vessel for Michael's pitch-perfect lament. Before I knew it the fedora went stage left and I glided stage right. I had to land the next move like an Olympic gymnast, a 360-degree spin that ended with me on my tiptoes. It happened so fast I barely had time to think, but I nailed it. The room erupted with hoots and hollers. Then I put one foot back, thrust my neck forward, and as the music hit the crescendo, muscle memory kicked in and all I had to do was bring the swagger. I walked forward and glided backwards. It couldn't have been easier.

I was an Indian, English kid who had been transplanted to America, dancing on a Tampa high school stage, channeling a black man who looked like an Indian girl. My grandmother was sitting in the audience and there was no turning back. It is true that you can't be Michael Jackson all the time, but on that day, for four minutes and thirty seconds, the entire student body—black kids, white kids, the jocks, the prom queens, Roy, Rick, the drama kids, and even the two Asian kids and Dilip—stood up and screamed, "Michael!"

BORN AGAIN

IT WAS HER HAIR THAT I FIRST NOTICED. A giant mound of brown curly hair surrounding a small, thin, alabaster-skinned face, punctuated by penetrating hazel eyes. Flirtatious one moment and aloof the next, they had a paralyzing effect on me the first time I saw them as I walked into the administration office on the second floor of the School of Theater building where I was getting my undergraduate degree, and where she was the brand-new Tuesday and Friday receptionist. Based on her clothes and her poise and the way she smelled, I imagined, in my limited experience with women, that she was older than me and the bubblegum-scented girls who ran around the sun-drenched University of South Florida campus.

I didn't know what she was studying, but it was clear that she was not one of us. She was not walking around with a copy of Aristotle's *Poetics* nonchalantly protruding from her back pocket, she didn't smell of cigarettes and coffee, she didn't wear sweatpants, and proudly not wash her hair because it was what the "character" required. She didn't over-enunciate or feel the need to pick up a guitar and start playing "Stairway to Heaven" during free periods, and she had probably never felt the need to narrate the progress of her bowel movements with improvised Shakespearean verse to the person in the next stall over: *Oh that this too, too solid flesh would melt, thaw, and resolve itself into a . . . poo*. In other words she was not a student of The Theater. If she had any of her own obsessions, they were quietly hidden behind a rather unassuming demeanor. She possessed the sophistication of a grown woman, with a kind of self-assuredness that I had rarely encountered before.

I decided I had to know her better. I also knew that she was far out of my league. I say "out of my league" implying that there were women who were actually in my league. The truth is I was eighteen years old and what most people would call a late bloomer. My father often drove this point home by reminding me of the fact that even in birth I had arrived two weeks past my due date, as if seeking an apology from me because his joy at having a firstborn son had been forever tarnished by my tardiness. To make matters worse, my initial lateness seemed to throw off everything in my life by several years. I was late potty-training, crawling, walking, and learning to ride a bicycle; and I was especially late when it came to girls. Of course, when I say girls, I mean the art of talking with girls and when I say talking with girls I mean flirting with girls, and when I say flirting with girls I mean knowing the difference between actually flirting versus buying coffee beans every week just so you can talk to the girl who works at the coffee counter in the mall, even though you don't drink coffee that much or know how to operate a coffee grinder. But you now have so many bags of coffee beans in the trunk of your car that your friends think you might be an over-caffeinated kleptomaniac.

Anyway, by the time I got to college, unlike my bohemian theater counterparts, who I assumed had had so much sex already that they found the very talk of it passé, I was still very much a virgin. In fact, I had never even really properly kissed a girl.

Being sent by my parents to a British all-boys boarding school at the tender age of thirteen hadn't helped in this regard, nor had the fact that I grew up in a South-Asian Muslim household with very conservative views of relations between the sexes. For many years as a child, back in England, I thought I might be going to hell for looking at my father's secret stash of *Penthouse* magazines. His magazines were the second place I had ever seen a naked female. The first was in elementary school back in England when I sheepishly touched Katie Ashcroft's vagina. This was an awkward and altogether unimpressive experience, especially considering that Katie hadn't exactly singled me out for this peer-pressure-fueled favor.

It was common knowledge that Katie regularly invited boys into the school bathroom and lifted up her skirt to show off her prepubescent vagina for reasons only she understood. The boys would line up outside the girls' bathroom and go in one at a time, which, surprisingly, never inspired an inquiry from the adults in charge. With her tinted glasses, pageboy haircut, and school uniform, Katie was normally a quiet, somewhat mousy girl who resembled Velma from the Scooby-Doo cartoons. But in that bathroom setting, as the dim afternoon light flooded in over the toilet stalls, she seemed to gain the sexual confidence of a Playboy Playmate.

"Are you ready?" she asked me.

I froze.

"Are you ready?" she said again, nodding at me with increasing impatience.

I nodded back politely.

"Well, take your hands out of your pockets then," she commanded.

I did as I was told although I didn't want her to see that they were moist and clenched.

"Don't be nervous," she said as she lifted up her plaid skirt and pulled down her underwear.

There it was. There was Katie Ashcroft's vagina. Unimpressive, I thought. That's it? Seriously? This is why every boy in school is lined up outside the girl's bathroom? To touch a crease? Was I missing something here? It looked so ordinary.

I don't know what I had expected. Perhaps that my senses would go into overdrive at the sight of her vagina, that I would suddenly be overcome with uncontrollable stirrings and urges that I had never experienced before. The truth was that I was underwhelmed and disappointed.

"Do you want to touch it?" she asked after I had stared expressionlessly for a few moments. Her voice now had a hint of vulnerability. Perhaps she'd noticed my utter lack of enthusiasm.

"Umm, okay," I said. I reached out and touched it in the same manner that I had recently touched a wounded baby sparrow that had fallen out of our neighbors' tree on top of our garage: with a level of reservation, frightened that the creature might suddenly decide to attack me. Katie's vagina did not attack me. Unlike the wounded bird that had twitched and shivered, it made no movement at all. It seemed lifeless and unaware that it was even being touched.

Katie's sad vagina constituted my entire experience of physical intimacy with girls until college. Armed with that disturbing memory and a trunk load of stale coffee beans, I ventured forth into the world of seducing Diane.

That was her name. I had overheard someone calling her that and made a mental note. I was afraid to actually use her name for fear that she might think I was stalking her since we had never been formally introduced. I found reasons to make copies whenever Diane was working, and eventually I was able to get her attention and even elicit an occasional smile with such classic pickup lines as "Excuse me, this copier is not working," or "Hi, sorry to bother you, but how do you change the size of the paper on this?" There was also my all-time favorite, the wildly enthusiastic "Hello!" I had many variations of this to draw on. Sometimes I went with the high-pitched "Helluuu!" On other occasions I shifted to a lower register, offering a deep-throated "Hellowwww," at times tinging it with a British accent, "Ello, ello, ello." Now and then, for the fun of it, I would just mouth the word "yellow" without making a sound.

All of this displayed a level of perseverance that she apparently found irresistible because after several months of strategic seduction, during which I copied the same scene from *Anthony and Cleopatra* twenty-three separate times, employed forty-eight differently accented hellos, twelve different goodbyes, and one attempt at physical comedy which I never repeated, where I pretended to bang my head into the door as I opened it, *she* asked *me* out on a date. This could not have worked out better. It had become clear that I needed women to make the first move for one reason: I was terrified of them.

My first exposure to women after the onset of puberty was in boarding school, where we had a populace of two hundred boys and six girls. Girls were only admitted starting in the lower sixth form, at around sixteen years old, no doubt to teach a bunch of juvenile barbarians who had spent the better part of their school life freely expressing their teenage male aggression to morph into proper English gentlemen before being thrust out into the real world.

The six young women in the school quickly realized that they had become the subject of every boy's sexual fantasies, and whether they liked it or not, they wielded an unnatural amount of power. In order to survive and to protect themselves from the onslaught of burgeoning male hormones, they cultivated a necessary detachment, aloofness, and even contempt. Females therefore to me were not earthly creatures. They were more like extraordinarily beautiful princesses who roamed the halls with shiny hair, dressed in brightly colored sweaters and who could, with a mere flutter of an eyelash or an askance look, grant you permission to live, or a reason to die. You can imagine how flattered I was therefore that, years later, just such a princess had asked me to accompany her to something, even though in this case that something happened to be church.

Most guys might have been turned off by this, but not me. The Methodist boarding school my Muslim parents had chosen to send me to required religious studies (i.e., Bible studies) plus chapel every Sunday. I was quite familiar with church. In fact, since there is no separation of church and state in the UK, even secular British schools would begin the day with a form of Christian worship. I was actually more familiar with Christianity than I was with Islam, the faith I was born into. Even today, I probably know more about the Gospel according to Mark than I do about any sura in the Koran. This is not a complaint. My mother and father, as good immigrants are wont to do, scrimped and saved to send me to one of the best educational institutions in the north of England. However it does seem to me there must have been a tacit agreement between my parents and the highly-accredited institution that in exchange for the prestigious opportunity and the education the school was providing, my parents would turn their heads while their son was being introduced to the teachings of Jesus Christ.

It didn't matter at all to the school which religion you had been raised in. There were students who came not only from Christian, but also from Muslim, Buddhist, Jewish, and even—God forbid—Roman Catholic families. But every Sunday we would all open our hymnbooks, raise our voices, and sing with a truly assimilated sense of apathy. All of this is to say that when Diane invited me to join her for church service, I wasn't the least bit put off; rather, I praised Jesus like a missionary intoxicated with the Holy Spirit.

Diane told me that Wednesday nights were youth nights at her church. As I stood next to the copier pretending to review my schedule, she went on to tell me that the entire congregation would be filled with young Christians in their teens and twenties who were all on fire for Jesus.

"That's great. I think I can make it," I said, trying not to nod too eagerly. She could have said Wednesday nights are when we all drink cat blood and sacrifice a small child and I would have responded the same way.

"You'll get to meet Brian, our youth minister. He's so charismatic! And after the sermon there might be a band. It's so much fun. You should meet me there."

"I will," I said. "I will. I definitely, absolutely will."

The church was a large modern building located on the north side of Tampa, and the first thing I noticed when I went inside, besides all the white faces, was the energy. It bore no resemblance to the quaint hymn-mumbling Methodist chapel I had attended back in my English boarding school days. The air was electric and everyone seemed charged with a purpose. I located Diane and walked over to sit next to her. She seemed transformed, unlike I had ever seen her before. At the theater building she always seemed somewhat reserved, mysterious, detached. Here she was smiling from ear to ear. She seemed softer and more approachable.

"I'm so glad you came," she whispered into my ear as I sat down.

For the first time I saw no sign of her usual dismissive eye roll, as if to say, "You are such a clown, Aasif." To my astonishment, she was looking at me with genuine fondness. I had come to the place where Diane could finally reveal *her* obsession, her passion, her secret: this church full of neatly-pressed white people. She was sharing something she loved with me.

Going all the way to back to my boarding school days, while I had to acknowledge that Christianity had many wonderful things about it—its inherent message of peace and forgiveness is difficult to argue with—the whole concept of Jesus being the Son of God had somehow never sat well with me. Perhaps it was because I grew up in a culture where Christianity was seen as the faith of the Caucasian man. Since Jesus the Son of God was always depicted as a white Anglo-Saxon, God himself must also be a white Anglo-Saxon. Although it was never something that my parents specifically taught me, growing up navigating between South Asian and Western cultures had made me acutely aware that we were very different from white Anglo-Saxons. Most of my parent's friends were South Asian—descendants of those who had been colonized and subjugated two generations earlier—and it was hard not to be aware of the contempt they had for white Anglo-Saxon culture when listening to conversations around the dinner table.

I clearly remember learning very early on that while Anglo-Saxons were running around in caves wearing animal skins, our ancestors were living in palaces, wearing silk, and inventing the alphabet. Anglo-Saxons drank too much and discarded their elderly when they became a burden, they were cold and emotionless despite their outward smiles, and they were racist and fearful at their core. They would eat anything, were unhygienic, and lacked a sense of culture or tradition. However, the thing to be wariest of was their insistence that God had a Son who was also a white Anglo-Saxon and if you didn't worship him, you were someone to be pitied, prayed for, and/or conquered. Sitting in this North Tampa Church of Jesus Christ next to Diane I knew therefore that I was a very unlikely candidate for conversion to Christianity. But the power of Christ works in mysterious ways, and I could not disregard the converting power of Diane's hypnotic hazel eyes.

During the next few months, I spent as much time with her as she'd let me. Together we went to church gatherings and Bible group meetings and socialized with friends of hers who were youth ministers and Christian camp counselors. I even found myself singing along to lyrics by bands like Petra and Stryper at the top of my lungs after she introduced me to Christian rock. This is a style of music that retains the throbbing bass line and screaming vibrato of traditional rock music but replaces the lyrics about sex, drugs, and rebelliousness with lyrics about salvation and morality. It was an odd yet effective form of marketing, a truly American approach to take the devil's music and rebrand it with Christ. Christian rock was an oxymoron, I thought to myself, an absurd notion, much like Christian pornography, but that didn't stop me. I was speaking in tongues to myself, convincing myself that I could successfully feign an interest in a churchgoing life, maybe even genuinely adopt it as my own belief system as long as Diane kept smiling at me . . . and my parents didn't find out.

Both Diane and I prayed earnestly to the cross, though while Diane's hung high on the church wall in front of us, mine hung on a silver chain between her perfectly shaped breasts. From what I could tell, however, except for occasionally ogling the scantily-clad underwear models on the cover of *International Male* catalog, which she claimed was under her coffee table because her roommate got it, she seemed to have no interest in exploring physical pleasures. No matter how much time I spent with her, she seemed only interested in a spiritual salvation.

As I got to know her better I discovered that Diane had turned to Jesus after an overindulgent adolescence. She had spent her teens doing drugs, dating bikers, and getting arrested, while I had spent mine doing school plays, watching movies, and going to the mall. It became clear that I was trying to win Diane for the exact opposite reason she was trying to win me.

It was as if I was finally ready to appreciate Katie Ashcroft's vagina—but with the wrong girl. Diane kept her vagina quite well hidden from me, as she did her breasts, her arms, her legs, and even the nape of her neck. In fact it was soon clear that Diane's entire physical body was off-limits. What she was really looking for from me was a friend in Christ. The only fantasy she was hoping to fulfill was to lead another soul to the Kingdom of Heaven. There were times I became so desperate, I would flip through back issues of *International Male*, feigning interest in the latest boxer brief designs just so that she would look over and I could possibly catch a glint of lust flash across her eyes like an accidentally exposed nipple.

After a couple of months of yearning and hoping, I managed to become friends with all of Diane's Christian friends. I was even able to impress them with my ability to discuss such issues as the controversy over whether, as per the Bible's Latin translation, Jesus had actually walked *on* water or merely *by the side* of the water, or whether the young man hiding in the bushes in the garden of Gethsemane during Jesus's arrest by the Roman soldiers, mentioned only in the Gospel according to Mark for some reason, is actually Mark writing about himself. Truth be told, I was merely parroting the few things I had managed to absorb from the curriculum of my religious studies class at boarding school. I was surprised I had retained anything at all since I actually spent most of the class carving images of naked ladies into the side of my wooden school desk. This was becoming a pattern, it seemed, for once again, here I was, discussing fellowship and abstinence all afternoon with Diane and her friends while simultaneously fantasizing about a naked woman's body. Christianity, it seems, makes me horny.

Perhaps in some mysterious way, however, Jesus was winning me over, for the idea of trying to win the heart and body of an alabaster-skinned Christian beauty by faking being a Christian had started to feel distinctly unchristian. This need to seduce her was either an unconscious pathology inherited from my subjugated ancestors or Diane was indeed the most beautifully and sexually inspiring creature I had ever met. Perhaps both things were true. Perhaps both things would always be confused. Perhaps it is a legacy of imperialism and slavery that the descendants of the conquered will forever need to possess the crusader's daughter.

It was upon this realization that something began stirring inside of me. I had a genuine epiphany: even though I had no intention of becoming a devout Christian, perhaps there was another religious route to gaining Diane's affections, one that could leave me with a little more integrity. I would come clean. I would reveal my true self to Diane. I would become a born-again Muslim.

In my sexually-frustrated near-delusional state this lightbulb moment made more sense to me than it would have to a less desperate guy, but truth be told there were some pretty good rationalizations to back me up. Islam and Christianity are essentially siblings, being born of the same root religion of Judaism. The prophet Mohammad (Peace Be Upon Him) met many Jews and Christians while travelling as a merchant throughout Arabia. From Jews he borrowed strict laws and discipline, and from Christians he took its view of a loving and forgiving God. The more I thought about it the more I could see that many commonalities bound the faiths together. Armed with this sense of religious communion, I decided to raise this as a discussion at our next Bible study meeting.

"Maybe I could read passages from the Koran to discuss in the same way we discussed passages from the Bible?" I inquired as we were wrapping up that day's discussion.

I waited for their response with a guileless expression. Diane and her friends stared at me, then at each other, looking for clues as to what the Christian protocol would be in a moment like this. I realized they were at a loss because the point of inviting me to these Bible study meetings had been to introduce me to Christ, not to have me introduce them to Mohammad.

After a long pause Brian, the youth minister, smiled and said, "Sure, that'd be great."

With that, I began what I am pretty sure was the first-ever reading of the Koran at the Young Floridian Christians on Fire

Bible study meeting. Diane and her friends listened attentively as I narrated the Koranic version of the birth of Christ (I figured I would start with somewhat familiar territory), where Mary alone (no Joseph, wise men, or shepherds) gives birth to Jesus under a tree with only dates for sustenance, and Jesus's first words are from the cradle saying, "I am indeed a servant of Allah, he hath given me revelation and made me a prophet."

When I was through, I looked up at their faces. Diane was smiling from ear to ear, as were her friends.

"I'm so glad you suggested this!" said Brian. "I have many thoughts about the similarities and differences between the faiths."

"That was fascinating, Aasif," Diane agreed, looking rather impressed and relieved. "I think you coming here every week and bringing us your faith is a tremendous idea."

Everyone else nodded in agreement. Had my crazy idea actually worked? Would I finally have sex with Diane not by pretending we were alike, but by accepting that we weren't?

For the next two weeks I basked in the bliss of having achieved a true spiritual union with Diane. The more discussions I led, the more I could discern a shift in Diane's attitude toward me. She began to single me out for my opinion on things and laugh really hard at my jokes. I noticed she was suddenly wearing more makeup, had gotten a new haircut, and was wearing outfits that were far more revealing than I had ever seen her wear before. On several occasions I even caught her looking at me out of the corner of her eye. It had worked. Praise Jesus or Mohammad or both of them. Maybe for once they were actually working in tandem. Perhaps, inspired by my work here on earth, they'd decided it was time to put aside their differences and help make one boy's sexual fantasy come true. Praise Jesusammad!!!

I don't think Diane even understood why or how, but it was clear that she wanted me, that some emotion was boiling up inside of her. Perhaps the Islam thing made me seem dangerous, forbidden, like one of those biker dudes from back in the day. I was *infidel-icious* and finally in the driver's seat. Armed with the knowledge that I could probably get Diane to go to second base, I went back to her apartment one Sunday to make my dreams come true.

Diane went into her bedroom and I stood outside it. I listened as she rhapsodized about that week's Bible study and how interesting my reading of the Koran had been. That she had no idea that Jesus was considered by Muslims to have traveled during his twenties to what is modern-day Iraq. I followed her, nodding and agreeing, and then I did something I'd never done before: I entered her bedroom without being invited. Standing there in the early evening light, Diane looked especially beautiful, her hair hanging loose. Leaning against her dressing table she masked her surprise at seeing me in her room with an overly casual demeanor. We both stood there silently smiling at each other. I froze. My hands were clenched and sweaty in my pockets just as they had been many years before with Katie in the bathroom.

"What's up?" she asked.

"Oh, nothing . . . just, you know," I mumbled.

We stood there for a moment longer, staring at each other, waiting.

"Hey, do you want to see *Dirty Dancing*?" she said suddenly. "I love Patrick Swayze."

She quickly brushed by me, back into the living room.

As she did, I glanced down at her bed and saw peeking out from under her pillow the most recent issue of *International Male*. Staring at me from the front cover was a photograph of a muscle-bound tanned model in a mesh thong with a sculpted chest, perfect biceps, a stubbled chiseled jaw line, deep brown eyes, and long flowing shoulder length blond hair. Behind him the sunset formed a halo around his head as he smiled, and in perfect Spanish said, "Hola mi amigo, me llamo Jesus, y ella siempre sera mio."[4]

I nodded my head as I agreed to get the popcorn.

---

4. Hello my friend, my name is Jesus, and she will always be mine.

THE CHILI PEPPER

AT THE AGE OF SIXTY, my father was fired from his part-time job as a Verizon customer service representative for using profanity. Even though she had heard him swear before, my mother was outraged and couldn't believe he would use such language at any time for any reason in a professional setting.

"Why does your father have to use such bad words?" she remarked while sitting in her armchair reading her copy of the Koran, as she did most afternoons. "The rest of the people who work there are young enough to be his grandchildren; what kind of example is that setting?"

But I was secretly proud of him. Not because he swore, but because of the reason he did so.

Let me first say that I am a huge fan of profanity. I know many people consider it to be coarse and uncivil and I would agree with them in most cases, but it can also be one of the most powerful tools we humans have to express something that cannot be expressed in any other way. Profanity is the chili pepper of language. If used by an idiot or a clod, it can overwhelm the discourse so the meaning is lost, but if used by a linguistic master chef, it can insert a piquant passion to the point where even though your ears may burn and you may want to rinse your mouth out, you cannot say it doesn't sound delicious.

Now, it was not out of character for my father to swear—he has used profanity for as long as I can remember, but only at home with us, his family. He would often mispronounce the swear words, much to the amusement of my sister and myself. He could rattle off quite a tiger-like roar of curses in Gujarati or Hindi, such as *bhen-chod* (sister-fucker), *madarchod* (mother-fucker), *gadhero* (donkey), and *buckwaas* (bullshit), but his command of English profanity was less sure-footed. More often than not he would end up stringing together the wrong words: "I am shitting on you" or "I will fuck your shit" or "Bloody shit damn." It would just make us laugh, which was clearly not the reaction he was attempting to elicit. Sometimes he would just shorten it to "shit damn," which means even less. You wouldn't really call someone a "shit damn," though I suppose there could be such a thing as an actual shit dam that keeps a river of shit from flooding a nearby town. Perhaps my father was referring to the great shit dam that lays somewhere out in the American West, an ecological eyesore where he intended to throw the lawn mower he was yelling at, or where he would like to send my sister and I when we used up all the hot water and he was forced to begin his day shivering naked under what felt like the receiving end of an ice cold shit dam.

In spite of all that, I had never seen him swear in front of his customers or his colleagues. During all the years that he stood behind the counter at his newspaper shop or grocery store back in England, cursed out by drunken skinheads and called a Paki and a wog and told to go back to his country on a daily basis, he never shouted back at them. Perhaps after they had left he called them bastards or *gadheros*, but only once they were out of hearing distance. Even after coming to America, when he and my mother would travel up and down the East Coast selling cheap Indian costume jewelry on the flea market circuit, he kept his cool. Often, because of their brown skin and exotic clothing, customers assumed they couldn't speak English and would speak to them like they were deaf children.

"WHAT IS YOUR NAME?" they would scream.

"Fatima and I speak English," my mother would reply, attempting to head off any misunderstanding or embarrassment.

The customers would look relieved and say something like, "Well, good for you. So many other Mexicans won't learn the language."

In spite of all this, I never heard my father lose control. This was, of course, in large part due to the fact that my mother was incredibly charming and a master salesperson. She could, with a disarming joke delivered with a self-deprecating laugh, get even the nastiest redneck to buy jewelry his wife would never wear, while simultaneously convincing him he might learn something by reading the Koran. This made it possible for my father to bite his tongue and sit quietly as my mom's second fiddle, telling himself that if he ever did say what he thought, he would go too far, say too much, and more important than losing his dignity or my mother's patience, he would commit the greatest act of sabotage and lose a customer.

So it was ironic that after twenty years of living in this country, during which time he ran several failed business ventures including an import-export business, an auto paint shop, and a multilevel marketing business, my father found himself having to use the English language as his primary tool when he took a job as a customer service rep. He used to joke that he would be perfect for the job: After living with my mother for more than three decades he had become an expert at listening to people complain. Truthfully, it was the most relaxed he had been in many years. He seemed glad to be away from the expectations and stress of owning a business, and he was content to be a voice on the other end of the telephone, a problem solver. He had never really had a penchant for business; his talents would have been far better suited to being a doctor, or a mechanic, a plumber, or even a musician. He actually taught himself how to play the harmonium and many times when I was in high school he would sit on the floor in the evenings, shirtless, his tanned belly hanging over his shorts like some kind of Florida Buddha and play tunes from old Bollywood classics. He was a pretty good singer and if it had not been for years of smoking when he was a young man, he would have perhaps kept the sharp pitch of his melodic voice.

When he was not singing, he was working in the garage, fixing the car, or cooking. Often happy to step up when my mother was too tired to cook, he would whip up some sub-continental concoction that was both mouth-and nose-watering. My father loved spicy food; he would in fact often eat raw chili peppers. Not swallow them whole, so as to avoid the burn, but actually bite into them and masticate them to mush.

At Verizon, my father worked in a small cubicle where he took about thirty to forty calls per shift. When the call that would be his last came in, it was halfway through his shift and it began like every other call: with someone upset that they were being overcharged, or someone claiming they never made any calls to Maine, or someone whose call kept getting dropped, or someone not understanding what the extra charges on their bill were for, or someone wanting to talk to a supervisor, or someone claiming their five-year-old had made these calls by accident, or that their teenager had visited those websites without permission. Whatever the complaint, the customer service representative's job was to stay calm and problem-solve. Periodically the supervisors would listen in on random calls, so you never knew when you were being evaluated.

This caller's name was Carl, and he was already upset that he had been kept on hold for as long as he had. My father apologized for the wait, to which Carl informed him he had to get to work and didn't have time to be sitting here dealing with this shit. My father said he understood and asked Carl for his account number, however, Carl didn't seem to understand.

"Can I have your account number?" my father repeated.

"I can't understand what you are saying," said Carl.

My father attempted to speak more slowly, but it didn't help.

"I'm sorry," Carl interrupted, "Your accent. I can't understand your accent. Look, I don't have time for this. Honestly, why can't Verizon hire people who can speak English?"

"I am speaking English," my father said, "and I need to know your account number."

"What is your name?" Carl inquired.

"My name is Hakim."

"Shit," said Carl, "have I been transferred to someone in India or Pakistan or some Arab country? I can't understand what you are saying and honestly I don't have time for this. I have called three times about this and I just need to get this bullshit resolved. I didn't make any calls to Palo Alto, wherever the fuck that is. I keep getting these charges on my account and I just want to talk to someone who I can understand, someone in my own fucking country, someone who I can trust, someone like me, someone who is an American. Now can I please talk to an American?"

"I am in America," my father replied, "I am in Tampa, Florida, and you can trust me. I work for Verizon and I can deal with your problem."

"Well, I don't care where you are and honestly I don't mean to say I can't trust you. I apologize. I'm very frustrated and I really just want to talk to someone else. Not to be rude but can you please just transfer me to someone who speaks English?"

"I do speak English," my father answered. "You are assuming I am a foreigner, because I have an accent, but I am an American just like you."

"You don't know what I am assuming," came the reply, fast and furious. "Now I didn't want to be rude to you, but here's what *you* can assume. Assume my son died in Iraq, killed by one of your people. Assume that I work for the FBI and I can have you sent back to wherever you came from before you can say 'camel shit.' Assume I am the fucking president of the United States and I want to exercise my right in the land of the free to speak to someone I can understand. Am I making myself clear?"

There was a moment of silence as my father stared into his reflection on his computer screen.

"Hello? Hello?" Carl repeated on the other end of the line.

"No problem," my father finally responded. "Let me see what I can do."

"Thank you" said Carl. "I appreciate that, I just really need to get this resolved."

Objectively, it was a perfectly reasonable request, my father thought, one that could have been easily rectified. He looked up from his computer at the other operators smiling and conversing with customers. He could see Joan, the young woman who was working her way through college, and Mike the middle-aged dad who had been laid off from his job selling insurance. They were typical Americans, who could have handled this call with aplomb. There was also Barry the supervisor. He could hand the call to Barry—that would be the procedural thing to do in a situation like this, he thought. My father smiled, put his headset on, and pressed the button to take Carl off hold.

"Unfortunately, no one else is available to help you, so it's me or no one," he said.

Perhaps it was the anonymity of the experience, neither man needing to see the other's face, that allowed them to throw civility out the window and say what they said in the following five seconds.

"Listen, you lying raghead kabob-smelling shit-for-brains sand nigger," Carl's voice came back through the phone line, strong and rattling like machine-gun fire, "I want you to transfer me to your supervisor in the next three seconds or I will fly down to Tampa fucking Florida and kick your shit-stained ass back to the shithole you came from, do you understand?"

That's when it happened. It was as if one of those chili peppers my father had eaten all those years ago came up through his stomach, through his throat, and out through his mouth. With it, it brought the power of profanity and poetry together in a single moment, like an orgasm thirty years in the making. My father took a breath.

"Shit damn!" he yelled. "Fuck to you!" And he hung up the phone.

Barry, the twenty-something supervisor sitting a few feet away, dropped his headset and came storming out of his office.

"What happened? Why didn't you transfer the call, Hakim?" he asked. "If a customer is belligerent you just transfer the call to a supervisor, you know the rules. Under no circumstances is it okay to tell a customer to . . . to . . . whatever it is that you even said."

"I know," said my father.

"You know we can hear you, Hakim," explained Barry. "Why would you say something like that when we can hear you?"

"He called me dirty names," said my father.

"Yes, that's right, he did," Barry replied, "and that was not right, and we all understand, but under no circumstances, I mean no circumstances are we allowed to swear back at customers. It's policy. I mean, what would happen if we swore at everyone who called us names?"

"I don't know," said my father, "what would happen?"

"We wouldn't be America's number-one cell phone provider, Hakim. That's what would happen."

My father smiled in agreement. He knew what was coming next, and yet ironically he had not felt this good, this energized in many years.

"You realize this is grounds for termination?" asked the supervisor, trying to sound as authoritative as he could.

"Understood," said my father, still smiling as he collected his things.

"This is not a laughing matter, Hakim. The caller could place an official complaint. He might even switch to another provider. We might have lost a customer."

My father stood up and shook his hand.

"Thank you for this wonderful opportunity," he said.

"We are very sorry that we have to let you go," Barry replied. "I mean, unfortunately due to this incident I will be unable to give you a positive recommendation."

"I won't need one," said my father. "I am going into retirement."

"Oh, what will you do?"

"I'm going to grow chili peppers," said my father. "I'm going to grow hundreds and hundreds of chili peppers. The hottest fucking chili peppers anyone has ever tasted."

Then he picked up his belongings, walked through the exit doors, and disappeared into the humid Florida night.

LOVE, INDIAN-AMERICAN STYLE

THE MOST ROMANTIC THING my parents ever did during my childhood involved urine. I was not there when it actually happened. I was in rehearsal for a play at school, but the story has been told to me many times and has been recounted at many family gatherings over the years. It is the stuff of Mandviwala legend.

Like many South-Asian second-generation children my sister Shabana and I grew up seeing little or no physical affection between my parents. Unlike the parents of my Western friends, who seemed incredibly comfortable with outward displays of affection, pecking each other on the lips or calling each other "Sweetie" and "Honey" and "Darling," my parents never did any of that. If my father started a sentence with "Darling" or "Sweetie" it meant he was attempting to mitigate the fact that the content of the sentence was probably about to make my mother very angry. There were rarely impromptu flowers, there were never date nights, and if my father ever told my mother she looked beautiful, or she ever told him he looked handsome, it was done in the privacy of their bedroom or they were saying it for the benefit of their Caucasian friends. They were raised in a culture that valued collective duty over individual desire, in which marriage and family were not a romantic, individualistic venture. Perhaps this is why divorce is generally so infrequent in traditional South Asian homes. The purpose of marriage is not to make you happy or fulfilled—for that there is work, religion, friends, even Bollywood—the purpose is to create family.

There was love between my parents, but the devotion came from commitment, not romance, and love was shown through actions and sacrifice. They each had specific roles. My mother took care of the home and the children while knowing she could run my father's business better than he could. My father worked and brought home the money while knowing he could cook better than she could. They behaved like partners but rarely like friends. Except for on this particular evening.

Having grown up in a family that spent the majority of its time outside of the Indian subcontinent—we only visited our relatives back home about once every decade—my sister and I did not know very much about our homeland and culture. The only parts of Indian history that we knew about were: Partition, the British Raj, and the story of the Taj Mahal. We knew the names, like every other Indian kid growing up in the West, of those Indians who would be immortalized on India's version of Mount Rushmore: Mahatma Gandhi, Indira Gandhi, Jawaharlal Nehru, and Amitabh Bachan. However, the Indian historical figure we were most fascinated with was not that famous at all: Morarji Desai. In history books he is recorded as the former Indian prime minister who served for a mere two years from 1977 to 1979. But in our minds he loomed large, not for his political career, but because of a strange, and some might consider a dangerous, practice. He drank his own urine. Not once, by accident, but daily as part of a medicinal regimen that he swore by.

My sister and I first heard about Desai and his urine drinking from one of my uncles when we were visiting our cousins in Bahrain back when Desai was in office. The image of this old man drinking his own urine had completely captured our imagination. It was absurd and disgusting, though perhaps the strangest thing was that, when we told our parents, they were not more appalled.

"Don't you think it's disgusting, mom?" I asked.

"Well, beta, many people in India do those kind of things," she replied. "Who is to say?"

"The man has grown to be very old," said my father, "so who the hell am I to judge him? To each his own, I suppose."

Urine-drinking was one of those things that, as an Indian kid, you hope your friends never find out about your culture—bathing in the Ganges and cows in the middle of the highway are already difficult enough to explain to your western friends. So it was soon put aside as a topic of conversation, but my sister and I never forgot.

Many years after Desai was out of office, and after we had moved to America, my sister sat watching television one afternoon in our modest two-bedroom home. The bathroom door was to the right, just visible in her peripheral vision. She heard the toilet flush and soon after my father exited the bathroom with a glass of liquid in his hands. Clear yellow liquid. She looked at my father, puzzled, as he stood watching the television casually drinking his beverage.

"What are you drinking?" she asked.

My father looked at her for a moment, then glanced at the liquid and sighed.

"Do you really want to know?" he replied.

"Yes," said my sister, becoming ever more curious. She was beginning to suspect something very troubling.

My father sighed again and then uttered the word.

"Urine."

My sister leapt to her feet.

"What? Are you serious?" she squealed.

"Just calm down," he said. "It's not that big a deal, Shab."

"Not a big deal? Not a big deal? You are drinking your own urine! That is disgusting."

Questions came to her that she didn't dare ask. How long had he been drinking his own urine? How often had he planted a huge kiss on her cheek, telling her he loved her? Just last week she had shared half his ice cream. Not to mention the time that she had eaten his leftovers from the doggy bag of Chinese noodles. She began to itch uncontrollably.

"Mom!" she screamed.

Our mom ran into the living room to see what the commotion was.

"What's wrong, what happened?"

"Look what Dad is doing. Can you believe it?"

Mom looked at the glass of yellow liquid, looked at Dad, and said, "Oh, Hakim, are you drinking your urine again?"

My sister's jaw dropped to the ground. How long had this been going on?! As she looked on with horror, Mom reached over and took the glass.

"Well, Hakim, don't keep it all to yourself, let me have some," she said, and proceeded to take a big swallow. My sister started to dry heave.

"It's a little spicy," she said as she handed the glass back to Dad, "but it's actually not that bad."

Shabana could not believe what she was witnessing.

"Have you lost your mind?" she screamed. "What are you guys doing? That is disgusting!"

Our parents just looked at each other, puzzled.

"What's wrong, beta?" Dad asked. "People in India have been doing this for years. Remember Morarji Desai? He lived to almost one hundred! I mean, if it was good enough for him, then it's good enough for us."

My sister began to back out of the room, unable to process what she was witnessing, but our mother grabbed her gently by the arm.

"Come on, beta take a sip," she said. "We are family. It's fine. And besides, you don't want to hurt Dad's feelings. Are you really going to tell your father that his daughter thinks she is too good to drink his urine?"

My sister was speechless, unable to believe this was happening. Her own parents had turned into monsters right in front of her eyes.

"Now stop being difficult," mom insisted. "Just try one small sip, it's good for you."

"Aaaaaaghh," Shabana screamed, as they wrestled her onto the couch.

My mom held her down as my father brought the glass up to her mouth. Shabana shook her head frantically from side to side to escape the putrid liquid. Finally a few drops fell onto her lips. Bubbles of carbonation fizzed and popped into her nose and she smelled the familiar smell of Mello Yello soda.

"You guys are jerks!" she screamed. "I hate you!"

But it didn't matter. Our parents were overtaken with peals of laughter, both of them more proud of this practical joke/one-act play than they were of anything they had ever done together, including raising two children and emigrating. It was a moment of complete abandon. They turned to each other and did what we had almost never seen them do. They kissed each other. On the mouth.

My sister walked out of the room and went to her bedroom and slammed the door.

At this point, my mother has always claimed that my father turned to her and said, "Well done, darling. I never knew you could be so devious."

My father has always claimed that my mother winked at him and said, "You are a very bad man. Hiding your own bottle of soda in the bathroom from the kids."

My sister claims that while she sat sulking in her bedroom, she heard my father usher my mother into the bathroom and lock the door. There was the fizz of carbonation and they giggled and whispered like two teenagers raiding a cheap motel mini bar.

All I know is that when I got home later that evening, my parents were nowhere to be found. However, a note on the fridge read, "We went to bed early. There's a plate of food for you in the oven and some nice cold urine in the fridge. Love, Mom and Dad."

Part III

WELCOME HOME: THE EMPTY SPACE

IT WAS LATE AFTERNOON AS I STOOD peeking into the front window of my childhood home on Frensham Drive on the north side of Bradford. I thought I might say hello to the current owners, but since no one was home, I fleetingly wondered if saying "I used to live here" would be a sufficient excuse when the neighbors reported the presence of a potential burglar.

Though it was too dark to discern much more than silhouettes of furniture inside, my memory filled the rooms with the images from my past.

My mother, a young Indian wife standing in the kitchen with a rolling pin, slapping dough in her powdery hands making roti for that night's dinner. Her children, myself and my sister, watching *Top of the Pops*[5] on a brand new color television set. Their father and her husband wearily returning home from standing behind the counter of his corner shop on Great Horton Road all day. A few

5. *Top of the Pops* is the British version of *American Bandstand*.

years later he would return from a grocery store in Shipley and then later still, after having given up on those businesses, he would return weary from a long day as a door to door salesman driving his van around West Yorkshire selling plastic and paper bags to South Asian shopkeepers.

She would put a bowl of daal, some chicken with roti and rice on the table, and he would eat it. Often, as if having been starved for sustenance, he ate so fast that the food would lodge in his chest and he would inevitably motion frantically for one of his kids to get up from—TV—run to—kitchen—fetch—glass—water—so that he could breathe again. After everyone was fed and the house was clean, she would lay down with Tiger Balm smeared across her forehead, simultaneously attempting to battle and ignore the untreated hypertension that would lead to kidney disease and dialysis later in life.

I spent the entire morning walking around the city of my youth, visiting the haunts of my childhood. I had come home to this northern England mill town after two decades of living in America and ventured forth on a pilgrimage to touch again the people and places that had shaped me. As an adult, they had dissolved into gauzy memories often leaving me with a feeling of being untethered and disconnected from my past. In returning I hoped that perhaps I would be able to, in some way, reclaim a part of me that always felt missing, although what that was, I didn't really know.

I stood in the parking lot of my old school, trying and failing to generate a feeling of familiarity and warmth about the swings and slides I had played on as a boy. A teacher approached me, perhaps wondering about a grown man loitering outside a school, and asked me if I needed some help. I told him I used to be a student, expecting a delighted grin or slap on the back. But he just shrugged and walked off muttering, "Great, you and a thousand other people."

I stood outside my dad's old corner shop which was now a Halal butcher, taking pictures. The bearded blood-covered butcher came out holding a meat cleaver and asked suspiciously why I was taking pictures of him. I explained that this shop used to be named after me: *Asif's News Agency*. Instead of offering me chai, he seemed annoyed, but then mustered a smile and curtly said, "You have five minutes to look around, sorry, we are very busy, there's a big wedding tomorrow."

I walked up to the reservoir where my friends and I would go sledding in the winter, but the shimmering wonderland I recalled from my childhood was just a dirty and overgrown piece of municipal property looking out over factories and council estates. And now, here I was clearly trespassing by staring into someone else's windows and standing in someone else's front yard desperately looking for something that I could not even name, but felt bereft at not having found.

As I looked up and down the street I remembered how excited they had been about this small, unremarkable, semi-detached, red brick bungalow that sat unremarkably in the middle of an equally unremarkable subdivision. A lawn and a driveway, a fire place and an attic—it was certainly less cramped and much nicer than the tenement flat above his newspaper shop in a Pakistani ghetto. It was the American style upwardly mobile dream . . . in England.

She had grown up the feisty daughter of a well-to-do merchant family in India, her younger days filled with the finest clothes, jewelry, and lifestyle that could be afforded a young Dawoodi Bohra[6] Muslim girl.

She would often talk about the culture shock she experienced after emigrating, coming from a sheltered and chaste world where

6. A sub-sect of Shiite Muslims.

manners and propriety were everything and having to work in a television factory with young working class English girls who threw out racial slurs, smoked, cursed, drank, and talked openly about sex.

Perhaps had she been born the opposite gender or into a different culture, at a different time, she might have joined the men in her family and become a business mogul herself, for she certainly had the acumen. But forget CEO, or even flight attendant. She had had the audacity to secretly date a man whom her father deemed unsuitable, so dutiful wife was the only option for such a rebellious spirit. She was therefore soon married off to a more appropriate candidate.

For his part, he was a handsome, creative country boy, who loved painting and singing. He dreamed of becoming a doctor, artist, or musician; professions that would have been more suited to his tinkering and introspective nature. He was even accepted into medical school but was unable to go because his family couldn't afford it. Taking the lead from his wife's family, who saw success in business as the only source of masculine pride, he left his job in textiles at the local university, (which is the reason they ended up in Bradford in the first place) and became a small business owner. Embarking on a profession for which he had no passion or aptitude.

Their respective disillusionment meant that for many years thereafter she saw him as weak and he saw her as impossible to please. It was only in later years when she became ill and he was her caretaker, that their dysfunctional love story would blossom, as she would finally be willing to acknowledge his strength and he her sadness.

They struggled financially and money was always an issue. She dealt with it by being contemptuous but resourceful. She attempted to make her family's lower middle class life seem far more affluent, in part to keep up with her other Indian friends who were mostly doctors and . . . actually they were all doctors. But mostly she did this to maintain a personal aesthetic. There was nothing that she couldn't recreate better than what was on sale at Marks and Spencer's. Consequently this little house—from curtains to tablecloths, comforters to tea cozies, pillow covers, and lampshades—had been filled with her inspired and original creations.

He dealt with the frustration of failing at a profession he never desired and his wife's evident disappointment in him by being rageful and sometimes violent. Looking down the driveway I could still see him barreling out of the front door, chasing his son with belt in hand. Often she would run after them, leaving their five-year-old daughter crying in the house and try to stop him. As they would scream and fight on the back lawn for all the neighbors to hear she would grab his arm and scratch his face knowing all the time that it was not their son, but each other that they wanted to beat.

In that same backyard a few years earlier they had plucked out the hundred rose bushes beautifully planted by the previous owner. He claiming that he didn't leave India to tend to flowers all day and she claiming that her children needed a lawn upon which to play. So out came the fragrant blooming bushes that were soon replaced with square sods of grass, laid slapdash. They were left untended and were soon overgrown, resembling dozens of dead chia pets of various sizes.

It was here that their children were raised, playing, running and jumping on this broken, misaligned, transplanted earth. It was also on this sodding earth that their son discovered his penchant for imaginative wanderings and performing. Escaping the pall of disappointment and the din of anger that hung over their family, it was in this backyard where the world of imaginary wizards and wars, islands and pirates made up the seeds that sprouted into the desire to become a professional actor.

Upon hearing this from his son, he reacted by being passively unsupportive, mostly by letting her deal with their son's pestering entreaties and questions on how one could become an actor. At least he wasn't forbidding it, he thought to himself, the way his own father had done when he told him he wanted to go to art school. She was reminded of how she swore to always allow her children to have the adventures in life that she had been denied. To never deny them their passions, although she had naively thought that meant permitting them to go on school trips to Scotland or learning the piano.

"Acting is a hard profession beta, most people fail at it," she told her son. "Wouldn't you rather do something else?"

"No," he replied.

Based on a mother's intuition that her son's conviction might be real, she said, "Well then, in that case, why don't you write to local children's theater companies and ask them if they will let you act?"

How she knew that children's theater companies even existed was a mystery to her son, for it was not as if that their lives had room or excess income for the luxuries of theater. But without question he did exactly what she suggested.

She proofread each letter and added her own addendum that if they had any doubt as to her son's talent, they should know that he had received the most positive feedback from all the other kids' parents for his portrayal at seven years old of an Elf in the school play.

There were more than twenty letters. None of them received a reply, except for one.

The Brighouse Children's Theatre was located in a small town that was its namesake, almost eight miles away. They invited her son to come see one of the plays they were doing to determine if the life of a thespian was a true desire.

"If I told you that you could not go," she said upon receipt of the letter, "then what would you do?"

"I would be very sad," came the reply.

She held him in her arms and said, as if it was an incantation protecting against the vagaries of life, "Well, beta, I won't let you be sad."

In that moment, performing, writing, telling stories, being on stage, applause, lights, and audiences became his life. Her son transferred all that childhood backyard conjuring to the stage at the Brighouse Children's Theatre, and for the next three years before they all moved to America, some of the happiest, most creative Wednesday evenings of his youth happened in that modest little makeshift theater made out of an abandoned clubhouse.

Every few months they would put on a full blown production at a local town hall stage at which the parents, strangers in every other respect, would sit as peers in the audience and watch their children transform into characters from literature or fairy tales.

Perhaps she knew when she gave her son permission to join the theater that he needed its safe harbor, that in her son were rose bushes that she could not bear to see torn out. Whatever the reason was, the two of them would proudly come and see their son perform and from their seat in the audience, will his success on stage.

As I returned from my memories to the present, I realized that afternoon was turning into dusk and it was clear there was one place on my pilgrimage that I would be remiss if I didn't visit.

I took the number thirteen bus at the top of Hollingwood Lane, just as I had done every Wednesday night as a young teen, and as it weaved its way through the narrow streets that had been carved into the Pennine mountains, I could not imagine what the Brighouse Children's Theatre would look like today. Would it be populated with the same people that had been there twenty years earlier? I doubted it, but its image was frozen in time for me. We passed cobbled side streets, dry stone walls, graffiti-ridden park benches, fish and chip shops, and pubs, pubs, and more pubs, until the bus finally dropped me off in the tiny town of Brighouse.

I climbed the hill from the bus station as I had done so many times in my youth, but after more than an hour of walking around I realized that I was lost. The streets and the houses and the shops were all familiar to me, but I was completely turned around. I could not find the theater no matter how many turns I took.

Stymied, I walked into a pub that seemed like it might contain some helpful locals. There were a half dozen or so people sitting at the bar drinking pints, and a few old men playing cards in the corner. I asked the bartender if she had ever heard of the Brighouse Children's Theatre. She scratched her head and said she had not. She asked a few of the other people in the pub. No one seemed to know, until one gentleman asked me what the building looked like.

"It's a single story, wide, stand-alone building," I said, "with a porch in front where you can sit with chairs. It looks like, umm . . . a ranch."

"Bloody hell," came the response from a man sitting behind a pint. "It's J.R. bloody Ewing and he's lost his ranch."

The pub erupted into laughter.

"I don't know where you think you are lad," he continued, "but this is Yorkshire, not Dallas; there are no bloody ranches round here."

"Thank you," I said, smiling sheepishly, realizing that this seemed like the end to a rather disappointing homecoming.

I was about to walk out of the pub when suddenly a man from one of the back tables spoke up.

"Wait," he said. "It looks like a cricket pavilion."

"Yes! A cricket pavilion," I yelped. Why had I not thought of that?

There were nods of recognition all around, and some laughter as several people put their heads together and drew out a rudimentary map on a bar napkin.

After a five minute walk I found myself in a spot I had walked by a half dozen times before entering the pub. I was standing in front of a gate that separated me from a parking lot. I had not recognized it before because, to the left, where the theater should have been, was instead simply an open field. Still a bit confused and wanting to make sure I was in the right place, I stopped a woman walking by.

"Did there used to be a building here that looked like a cricket pavilion called the Brighouse Children's Theatre?" I asked her.

"Yes, I think they used to have theater classes here, but it burnt down almost ten years ago. It's just been this empty field since then."

"I see," I said as I stared motionless at the green field where once stood a place of childhood alchemy and magic. I stood watching the unmowed grass waving slightly in the chilly evening breeze. I pushed open the gate, ignoring the no entry sign and I almost felt like laughing as I stood in the middle of the damp field.

I had gotten on planes, and trains, and buses in this quixotic journey home, having embarked upon it hoping to find the talismans and codes that I believed would help me, once and for all, explain who I was, that would help me call someplace home. As though the story of personal identity and a sense of belonging were told in hieroglyphs and one just needed to find the Rosetta Stone.

So here I was, in this field. A baby born in Bombay, a boy raised in Bradford, a teenager transplanted to Florida, and a man living in New York. My story was not one of deep and longstanding roots. I would never be from the same place as my parents, or many of my friends. I would never have an accent or a personality marking me as indelibly from a region. I would never feel fully Indian or British or American. My story would never be lived on a wholly familiar plot of land. But I could lay claim to both ranches and cricket pavilions.

My home was the one I started building on this empty field where once stood a stage. It was a place of multiplicity where I could be anything, from anywhere, at any time. It was not made of bricks and mortar, or even the sum of memories; it was an act of creation in itself. Like my parents before me, I had to build it imperfectly for myself, whether from circumstance, fate, or necessity.

I stood smiling, knowing that I had come to Bradford looking for a home that I could touch, something that had existed in the past, but in its place I found the future, to be continually created and recreated and reinvented as I had done time and time again, from a bare stage, a blank page, an empty field.

As the sun began to set over the West Yorkshire skyline, I gathered my things, walked back through the gate, and decided it was time to get back on that bus.

PATANKING

Upon arriving in New York in the summer of 1991, I spent most mornings standing outside The Actors' Equity Building on 46th Street at 5 A.M. holding my headshot, my résumé, a cup of coffee, and a bagel, along with hundreds of other actors. We were all waiting to audition for an associate to the associate to the associate casting director for a role in . . . well, frankly anything. *Pippin*, *Death of a Salesman*, *Romeo and Juliet*, it didn't matter. I once even stood in line for four hours to be seen for a role in *A Raisin in the Sun*. It's not that I hadn't read the play—okay fine, I hadn't—but I had seen the movie. However, the one thing that kept me going as a young out-of-work actor was the belief that someday someone on the other side of the table would be so impressed by my monologue and/or sixteen bars of a song, that they might even be inspired to cast one really eager South Asian actor in a play about an African American family in the 1950s.

I guess it was also fair to say that there were not too many roles for South Asian actors, so although hoping to be cast as black, Latino, Native American, or Arab was a long shot, it was often the only thing available. Hey, I once played a Sephardic Jew for a murder mystery company and don't think I didn't put that in the special skills section of my résumé, because I did.

When I first arrived in New York, like everyone else, I was big on dreams and short on experience. For the previous two years, I had been working at theme parks in Orlando, improvising and doing comedy bits with the guests who came through the gates at Disney/MGM or Universal Studios. Other than that, when I first stepped off the train at Grand Central Station, my professional career consisted of a production of *Danny and the Deep Blue Sea* done in the backroom of a nightclub, a production of *Aladdin and his Wonderful Lamp* performed across the sunshine state for grades K through 3, an extra in an independent karate movie shot on location in Winter Haven, Florida, and one line on the TV show *Miami Vice* as the doorman outside the Biltmore Hotel. I acted the shit outta that line.

A couple of weeks after arriving in the city, I saw it as a sign that I had made the right decision when movie star and theatre legend John Malkovich exited a building and almost bumped in to me on West 46th Street. As Malkovich turned and walked toward 6th Avenue I stared at the doorway that he had just come out of. A sign above the door read The American Place Theatre. It was an unassuming building and the theater seemed to exist below street level. But it was clearly a place where movie stars hung out when they were not plastered on billboards and subway ads. This is where they go back to their roots, I thought, where they leave behind the high stakes business of the Hollywood box office for a period of time and reconnect to the simple magic of an actor standing on a stage in front of an audience telling a story. I decided that this was what I wanted. This was the door I wanted to pass through. From that moment on "being John Malkovich" became a symbolic mantra for me—until Spike Jonze stole my thunder a few years later.

The first item on my road to conquering New York was to get an agent. After eight months or so, I succeeded. I say that like it was an easy thing to do. It wasn't. I just don't want to bore you with the details of how to write a cover letter that is attached to a head-shot that could possibly make you stand out in the sea of a million other headshots and résumés (most of which end up in a trash can) that any actor competes against on a weekly basis in order to even get a single meeting.

My first audition was for a national television commercial. I was very excited since this could be a big payday, not to mention I was a terrible waiter. I was quickly discovering that even though I was living in a railroad apartment in Queens with a whole group of South American grad students, New York was still really expensive and it took a lot of time and effort to make just enough money to cover rent and food. A national commercial would solve a lot of my immediate problems. It was for the role of a snake charmer in a commercial for an insurance company (or possibly a bank). Either way, a snake charmer was an odd choice I thought, but why they needed one was not my concern, as long as they were going to pay me. I walked into the audition room and, after stating my name, I was asked to read some lines off a cue card while pretending to charm a snake out of a basket. I picked up the fake flute and pretended to play while I said the lines for the camera. After I was done the director conferred with his cohorts and then asked me something that seemed obvious to them, but took me by surprise.

"Could you do it again, this time with an Indian accent?" he asked.

Now, truth be told, I had never been asked to do an Indian accent before. Even though I had been born in India, I left as an infant and grew up in the UK and then in the U.S. where the coalescing of my West Yorkshire and Floridian accents made me sound like I was from Brooklyn. I wasn't even sure if I could do an Indian accent. The only Indian accent I had any reference to was my parents' and the last thing any immigrant kid wants to sound like is his father.

However, I was an actor and this was a paying gig, so I picked up the flute and gave it a go. It was terrible. I couldn't do it. I prided myself on being able to do most any accent; British, Irish, French, Italian, Hispanic, but for some reason I could not do an authentic Indian accent. I knew how it was supposed to sound, I had heard it all my life, but my mouth and voice refused to create the sound in my head. Like a tone deaf singer, I was Indian-accent deaf. I couldn't find the lilt, the upward inflection, the clipped consonants. I even wobbled my head from side to side the way Indians have been doing for thousands of years, hoping it would shake loose the accent buried inside of me, but no such luck. The words coming out of my face sounded like either an effeminate Russian or a very polite Arab, but definitely not an Indian.

To my surprise, however, the producers seemed unfazed.

"Well done, that was great," the director said.

"One more question," he continued after a moment. "Do you own your own turban?"

"Excuse me?" I asked.

"Our wardrobe girls don't know how to tie a turban, so if you happen to own your own turban . . ."

"I don't," I said, "I don't own a turban because . . . well because I don't wear a turban."

"Of course," he said, starting to sound slightly uncomfortable.

"If I owned a turban I would probably have worn it," I continued. "It's not something you leave home without."

I don't know why I was combative. Perhaps because I still couldn't believe they could not tell that I had just done the shittiest Indian accent ever heard. Did they not care? Didn't they know what an Indian accent was supposed to sound like? Seems like a pretty essential bit of information if you're casting a commercial featuring an Indian snake charmer.

"Of course," said the director, "that makes sense. We just thought. . . . Do you know how to tie one, because . . . ?"

"No, I don't," I said flatly.

That's when it got weird.

"Sorry to ask you this," one of the assistants piped up sheepishly, "but we are asking everyone. Do you know how to actually snake charm?"

"I don't," I said, "but I am Indian so it's probably in my DNA."

There was a pause.

"Of course," the director said. "Sorry. They are silly questions but the client insists. So let's do it again and this time don't worry about being too big, because we want this to be funny."

In most other auditions, this would have been at best an innocuous comment and at worst, just lazy direction, but I was beginning to realize he wasn't talking about being funny. He was talking about something else, something that was making me uncomfortable. I loved performing because it had always been a place where I felt freedom, acceptance, and expansion. In theater school, in plays, at theme parks, whenever I performed it had only ever brought me joy. But now, in this moment, for the first time, I felt something I had never felt before: shame. I knew that I was about to do something that my parents would be embarrassed to see. My stomach tightened as I imagined my friends attempting to be supportive and smile as they watched me on television doing this potentially offensive caricature. I thought for a moment. I could walk out. I could stand up and say, *this makes me uncomfortable. I didn't come to New York to be Apu. I came to . . . to . . . "being John Malkovich."* Which would sound a bit "Tourette's-y" I admit, but nevertheless would affirm my mantra and make a great exit line.

I stared at their faces, these nice, smiling Caucasian people, who had no idea what they were asking me to do. Then I remembered that rent was due at the end of the month. Would I once again ask my landlady for a little more time? Every month I gave her the same sob story. I remembered how much I hated waiting tables, I remembered that paralegal job where reading a three-hundred-page legal brief about faulty valves had actually made me consider suicide. I remembered that there were ten other actors sitting outside the door that would do this part, no questions asked, and laugh all the way to the bank. If I didn't do this on principle, one of them would, and then what difference would it make? What statement would I be making? Maybe if I did do it, I could have control over it. I could give this bobble-headed, snake-charming cartoon character some nuance, complexity, humanity. I mean for God's sake what was my problem? It was a fucking stupid commercial. I should just do it, take the money, and this time next year no one would even remember it. But I would know, I thought to myself. I would hate every minute of shooting it and I would spend the next few months before it aired feeling anxious and humiliated.

I stood up from the lotus position to confront them . . . and also because it's an incredibly uncomfortable way to sit for a long time.

"So, you want it to be broader?" I said to the director. "You want it to be more like a cartoon?"

"Well, we want it to be funny," they said as they looked at each other. "The accent, the head wobble, it all makes it funnier. We want it to be funny."

I looked at them in the eye took a deep breath and said, "Okay, I think I know what you want."

I sat down and assumed the lotus position. I wobbled my head from side to side. I channeled the broadest Indian accent I could think of by pretending to be Peter Sellers in *The Party*. I channeled Apu from *The Simpsons*. I even channeled Fisher Stevens in brown face from that '80s robot movie. I was actually trying to appear on national television doing the same accent that, if someone had done it in front of me, I would have punched them in the mouth.

The whole thing worked like a snake charm, for the more I did it, the more the producers smiled and soon they were laughing uncontrollably, especially when I smiled and stared at them as if I didn't understand what they were saying. I attempted to soothe my humiliation by focusing on how much money I would make by hitting what was clearly the brown cash cow jackpot.

"Dude, that was so funny," said the director when I had finished. "Thank you so much for being a good sport. I know it is probably a little politically incorrect, but it's comedy, right?"

"Of course," I said. "I totally get it. Anything for a laugh."

I did not get the job. I assumed that they had cast some other brown actor better studied in the art of snake charming, and to be honest part of me was relieved. However, when I saw the commercial a few months later I saw to my horror that they had cast a swarthy looking white guy. There he was, bobbing his head from side to side, smiling and talking with a broad, terrible Indian accent without a care in the world as to what his parents would think of him as he charmed the shit out of that rubber snake.

Though I was never asked to play a snake charmer again, I soon noticed a peculiar pattern in the roles I auditioned for—cab drivers, deli owners, doctors, and terrorists. As time went on I became more and more numb to what was being asked of me. My friend, Sakina Jaffrey, a South Asian actress, even coined a name for it: Patanking. The word is derived from parodying the sound of an Indian accent to the ear of a white person: "patank patank patank." Say it to yourself. Did you do it? (Yes, this part of the book is interactive.) Now try saying it with an Indian accent. Give it a shot. It doesn't have to be perfect. Did you do it? Now wobble your head from side to side. (This will be difficult if you are not South Asian since it's a motion that is confounding to westerners but is instinctively understood by anyone who has even one drop of subcontinental blood in their veins. Don't worry if you don't do it perfectly. You never will.) Okay, now that you are saying "patank patank patank" and wobbling your head from side to side like a dashboard bobble head you are experiencing what my first few years as an actor in New York felt like. (If you are laughing right now, you're a racist!)

Patanking was not just a dialect. It happened when an Indian character in a movie or a TV show or a commercial was void of any human element, and became simply a disembodied accent, head wobble, or turban. It was also sometimes the only way to make a living, and I was completely culpable for I gladly patanked my way as far up the ladder as I could.

Eventually I didn't even think about it. I gladly served up a one-dimensional cartoon of my culture and family for the entertainment of Middle America. I turned a blind eye to things that I could not justify, such as why a character born and raised in the west would even have an Indian accent. Why a character that was clearly Indian would be named Epstein. Why a Muslim character would have a Hindu name. Why an Indian would be speaking Arabic. Why a character originally written as black or Hispanic or Jewish could just as easily be played by an Indian without needing to change a single piece of vernacular. Why a tanned white actor could play South Asian, but a light skinned South Asian could not play white. Why an Iranian accent sounded identical to an Indian one. Why South Asian actors could be funny or nerdy but never sexy, yet South Asian actresses had to be. I got so used to twisting myself into a metaphorical pretzel in order to fit in to the way that Hollywood portrayed South Asian or Middle Eastern characters that I didn't even realize I was doing it.

But then something began to change. After playing countless South Asian stereotypes, I began to feel a need to create something real. If I was professionally not able to play anything more than a peripheral and undeveloped character (except for some reason in Shakespeare and in school, because apparently nontraditional casting is okay if the audience doesn't know what the actors are talking about or if it's for educational purposes), then I would tell those stories myself. I started writing characters from my ethnic and immigrant experience, in hopes of creating a one-man show. The characters were unlike any that I had ever had the chance to play. They were as complicated and conflicted as the people they were inspired by. For the first time the audience would not think,

"Look, nontraditional casting. Good for them, that's very progressive," when they saw me walk on stage, as they had in every play I had ever done. This time they wouldn't even notice. They would just see a South Asian actor portraying three dimensional South Asian characters. There would be no suspension of disbelief. Except for the usual kind.

With this in mind, I began to write what would become my one-man show *Sakina's Restaurant*. The first character I developed, Sakina, was a combination of me and my sister. I quickly realized that though the play would enable me to return to my roots, it would require me to do some nontraditional casting of another variety—I would have to play all ages and genders. So one of the first things I did was put on a pair of heels and a mini skirt and walk around my apartment to see how it felt to talk and walk like a teenage Indian girl.

After Sakina, I wrote a character based on my father and for the first time I tried to reveal him, rather than lampoon him. I attempted to give the character of Mr. Hakim an authentic immigrant voice, to uncover how he might actually feel about the emotional and cultural price he paid for his American Dream. I wrote a character based on my mother's experience of being a young woman seeking romance within an arranged marriage. I continued writing characters and eventually crafted an entire family made from bits and pieces of my relatives and others like them.

The last character I wrote was a South Asian Muslim medical student who has sex with a prostitute the night before his wedding. The monologue's literal and metaphorical climax involves the prostitute performing oral sex on him while he prays to God for forgiveness. I was very proud of it and so when my girlfriend at the time, an actress herself (no doubt sick and tired of coming home to the sights and sounds of her boyfriend either wearing heels or having loud sex with imaginary prostitutes), told me that Wynn Handman, the artistic director of the American Place Theatre, had an acting class and that I should audition for it, I leapt at the chance.

Wynn had helped develop the careers of hundreds of notable actors, but more important to me, he had helped develop the solo performance careers of monologue-makers such as Eric Bogosian and John Leguizamo. The prospect of auditioning for him was intimidating, but it was kismet that he also owned the same theater that I had seen Malkovich walk out of a few years earlier.

Upon entering his studio in Carnegie Hall, which was a small black box type space with about forty or so wooden seats raked up toward the back wall where the students would sit, I spotted Wynn seated in what I would come to know as "his" chair, off to the side, next to the light board. He was an older man in his seventies and he didn't seem to have a lot of patience. So after the perfunctory hellos he got right down to business.

"So what are you going to do for me?" he asked.

"I'm writing a one-man show," I told him. "I have written an original monologue."

"Okay, go ahead," he said with no enthusiasm whatsoever as he dimmed the lights in the studio.

"I have to take off my pants," I called as the stage went black. "It's part of the piece. I'm going to be receiving oral sex from a prostitute."

Wynn was silent. In the darkness I heard him shift his weight and sigh. Then, without a word, he slowly turned on one blue stage light, enough to see that he wouldn't have to call Carnegie Hall security. He saw me standing there smiling in my boxers with my pants around my ankles.

"Are you going to be removing any more of your clothing?" he inquired.

"No, just my pants," I responded.

"Tell me when you are ready to begin," he said and turned off the blue light.

I spent the next several years in Wynn's class honing and developing the characters I had written. Wynn gave me the tools to take my raw material and insert dramatic tension, to create real characters and not just mouthpieces for a point I wanted to make. He helped me shape my ideas into human beings. The act of revealing real South Asian characters on stage that were not caricatures or peripheral brown people in some white writer's POV but actually the focus of the story, was transformative and empowering and validating in a way that nothing I had done up to that point had been.

When I was finally ready, after workshopping the play in various downtown theaters, Wynn offered to premiere *Sakina's Restaurant* at the American Place Theater. It was 1998, almost seven years after I had gone to that audition for a snake charmer. I had been unable to appreciate or access my own accent and cultural identity when I first came to New York and now I was standing on a stage portraying a South Asian American family for a New York City theater audience.

As soon as word got out about the show, South Asian audiences came from all over the tri-state area. Many of them had never seen a story that reflected their experience, their culture, or themselves on stage before. It wasn't just South Asians, either. I was surprised to find how much Indian immigrants had in common with Greeks, Italians, Arabs, and even a family of Russian Orthodox Jews from Brooklyn. They came and kept coming, and a show that was supposed to run for two weeks managed to stay open for six months.

On the night the show closed, I walked out on to 46th Street and stood staring at the poster on the front of the theater for one last time. Suddenly I heard my name. I turned around and saw a lanky Indian kid in his early twenties.

"Hey," he said nervously. "I just saw your show. It was amazing and I wondered if you would sign my program."

"Sure," I said, and while I did he told me he was an actor and had just arrived in the city.

"My parents didn't want me to be an actor," he explained, "but I've wanted to since I was a kid."

"Great," I said. "I wish you the best."

"I played so many great roles in college," he continued, "but now, it's hard. I only get auditions to play stupid roles. I'm sick of only being a cab driver or your friendly neighborhood terrorist. It's so humiliating. How did you manage to avoid it?"

The question made me smile.

"Do you want to get a drink?" I asked as I handed the program back to him.

"Really?" He asked. "Are you sure?"

"Yeah," I said, "I don't have to be anywhere and I'd like to tell you a story."

"Sounds cool," he said, falling in step beside me. "What's it about?"

"It's a story I call *Patanking*."

MOVIE STAR

HE WAS HAVING SEX ON MY CHAIR and he broke it," screamed Ismail Merchant as he picked up the two pieces of wood that just moments before had comprised his priceless antique piece of furniture.

The entire dinner party turned to me, horrified. The same people that had been congratulating me for being picked to be the star of Ismail's new movie were now looking at me with confusion and disgust, as if I was some kind of ungrateful sex addict. The kind of person who would have the audacity to stay as a guest in someone's home and then repay them by having sex on—and breaking—their antique dining room chair. I stood in stunned silence staring at Ismail, not knowing quite how to respond.

I had met Ismail Merchant almost two years before, in 1998, during the run of my one-man show *Sakina's Restaurant*.

Several weeks into the run, the *New York Times* gave the play a superbly generous review. That night the manager of the theater ran excitedly down from her office while I was doing my vocal warmups.

"Guess who is coming to the show tonight, to see YOU?" she exclaimed.

My heart stopped for a minute. I had already been reeling all day from the review that had in twenty minutes that morning caused my answering machine to fill up with messages of congratulations.

"I don't know if I really want to know," I said. "Not right now, since I am about to perf—"

"Ismail Merchant!" she screamed. Then very fast and in one breath, "He'scastingamovieandhe'slookingfortheleadandheiscomingtosee YOUOhmyGodRemainsoftheDayismyfavouritemoviebutIdon'twant todisturbyousoI'msorrymaybeyoucanjustpretendlikeyouneverheard thatandbreakalegtonight . . . by the way it's sold out!"

Then she disappeared.

I looked in the dressing room mirror and remembered that eight years earlier I had attached on my bedroom wall a poster board on which I had written, in blue marker, that I would be a movie star by the year 2002. I felt nauseous.

Ismail introduced himself after the show. I was in the middle of a conversation with a couple of audience members when he interrupted with his signature bombastic post-colonial Indian lilt.

"My name is Ismail Merchant," he said with arms outstretched as if he were Moses triumphantly parting a very small group of people, "and I would like to take you to dinner."

A few days later I met him at an Indian restaurant he claimed he owned, although none of the waiters seemed to recognize him. As we finished eating he gave me a copy of a book called *The Mystic Masseur*.

"V. S. Naipaul," he said, "Trinidad's greatest author. This was his first book, set in Trinidad in the late fifties. Have you read it?"

I told him I had not.

"Well," he said, "you must absolutely read it immediately, because you are going to play the lead in the film I am making of this book."

Simple as that? I thought. Wow. I really should have written more stuff on that poster board.

"Now you really have to try the gulab jamun in this place," he said as he called the waiter over. "Manish, please tell the chef to bring us some gulab jamun."

Manish went to put in the order for our desserts after explaining that his name was actually Suvir. Meanwhile I stared at the glossy paperback cover of a book that I would read and finish that very night.

After that dinner, I did not hear from Ismail Merchant for a year. I eventually concluded that I had been taken out to dinner and offered the lead role in a movie as a practical joke by an incredible impersonator.

However, the following summer, after my show had closed and I was back to doing my most interesting work in acting class, I got a call from Ismail Merchant's secretary.

"Ismail would like you to go down to Twenty-Eighth Street and Lexington tomorrow and get fitted for a turban," she said.

"Excuse me?" I replied.

"They will see you tomorrow at 6 P.M."

"A turban?" I asked, infuriated. "No, I will not."

I had left Ismail many messages, none of which he had bothered to return, and I was not about to jump at his beck and call.

"I won't go," I continued, "unless I can speak with Mr. Merchant himself."

Before I could even finish the sentence, Ismail was on the line, speaking to me as if we had had dinner just the day before.

"Aasif, how are you?" he exclaimed. He sounded cheery and enthused. "Now you will be wearing a turban in the film for some of the scenes, so you must go down to this wonderful sari shop on the east side and they will fit you. The owner is expecting you."

"But are we even doing this film?" I asked. "The last time we spoke was a year ago and you've never even showed me a script."

"Are we still making the film?" he asked, seeming genuinely hurt by my lack of faith. "Of course we are making the film and you will have a script as soon as it's ready."

"Okay," I said, flustered. "It's just, I thought maybe the whole thing had fallen through."

The disappointment in my voice must have been evident because he reassured me that nothing had fallen through and principal photography would start in no time. I smiled with relief like I was speaking to an absent girlfriend who had told me she still loved me.

"Okay, so if this is happening then I am going to mentally prepare myself. I am going to invest," I said. I wanted to add, "So please don't fuck with me," but I didn't. Ismail's voice came through loud and clear in response.

"Invest! Invest! Invest!" he said.

I seem to remember the conversation trailing off, probably because I was so giddy that I don't actually remember hanging up.

After that conversation I did not hear from Ismail Merchant again for another six months. However, a script arrived by messenger a week later. For an actor who had mostly done theater or played the occasional shopkeeper or medical expert on shows like

Law & Order, I still could not fathom that I would be the star of a Merchant/Ivory film. As I read the script for the first time I don't think I even comprehended it. Turning the pages I found myself constantly distracted by the MANDVI watermark and simply marveling at the fact that my character continued to have more lines.

To calm my anxiety about having to carry a film and working with such Academy Award–winning talent right out of the gate, I decided my course of action was to become the consummate professional. I would access all that I had learned in school, all that I had learned from Wynn Handman, all the speech and vocal exercises I had ever done and hated doing. This was my moment and I could not afford to fail. I would become a master instrument.

I began by adopting a technique that Anthony Hopkins had said he used when approaching a role. He would read the script a hundred times before the first day of shooting; that way he knew the character inside and out. I made it to eighteen before rationalizing that Sir Anthony must have very little else to do in his life. I worked on various scenes in my acting class with Wynn, who did some character interviews with me, which is an exercise where an actor is interviewed while in character. Working on the role with Wynn made me realize a few things: I needed to spend more time listening to the dialect tape that Ismail had sent over to master the exact idiosyncratic specificity of the dialect; I needed to know a lot more about Trinidad's culture, its food, and its people; and I also probably needed to sign some kind of contract.

In my excitement and because Ismail only seemed to talk to me once a year I had never mentioned this project to my manager, Mike. Mike didn't have many clients. Actually, he had only one. He was the kind of manager who called me more than I called him.

So when I told him that I had been offered the lead in a movie, Mike was thrilled. Ismail was not.

"Ismail wants you to come to his office, right now," said Mike when he called a few days later. I had never been to the Merchant/Ivory offices and felt a pang of excitement at the prospect, but I also knew this was the result of nearly fourteen phone calls that had been made in three days between him and Mike regarding my per diem. Ismail had called and wanted me to fly to London for the weekend to be fitted for costumes but for some reason was refusing to pay for any food or lodging.

"What did you say to him?" I asked.

"The same thing I have been saying all week." said Mike, "If he wants you to go to London for a costume fitting, you need a place to stay and money for food. It's a reasonable request. I don't know why we are being met with such unimaginable resistance. You don't even have a fucking contract. I can't in good faith let you fly to London without food and lodging to be fitted for costumes for a movie that may not even happen."

My heart sank as I looked at the color-coordinated flowchart on my wall that tracked the emotional journey of my character in the course of the one-hundred-and-fifty-page script. The film spanned thirty years in the life of my character, Ganesh Ransumair. I had noted that there were nine major emotional turning points and seven extensive gaps in time, which I had filled in with my own imagination, and there were three scenes where I was really going to have to "bring it" and cry.

"So why do I need to go to his office?" I asked.

"I don't know, just go see what he wants," said Mike.

"I hate the son of a bitch," he added before he hung up.

As I walked into Ismail's office he gestured for me to sit in one of the two plush leather chairs on the other side of his giant desk. The desk overflowed with papers, fountain pens, exotic paperweights, and a stack of several copies of his most recent cookbook, hot off the presses, as if guests were obliged to buy one before leaving. He was on the phone arguing with James Ivory about the appropriateness of calling Harvey Weinstein an uncultured oaf.

"You can't say that to him, Ismail," I could hear James saying on the speaker phone, with a quiet fatigue in his voice that seemed borne from years of conversations just like this.

"I don't bloody care!" Ismail screamed. "The man is a pig. He's an uncouth animal. How dare he say that Merchant/Ivory only makes costume dramas. *A Room with a View*, *Howards End*, *Remains of the Day*, *Heat and Dust*, *Mr and Mrs Bridge*: They are films about character and story. If he is interested in costumes, he can jolly well go down to the Metropolitan Museum of Art and look at costumes all day long."

I glanced around as he spoke. The office was like a gallery of accolades with BAFTAs, Oscars, and Golden Globes placed conspicuously throughout the bookshelves behind me. The walls were decorated with pictures of himself and Jim in younger days with the likes of Madhur Jaffrey, Vanessa Redgrave, Julie Christie, Shashi Kapoor, and Anthony Hopkins. I sat in silence for almost fifteen minutes while he screamed and gesticulated. Finally he hung up and, without missing a beat, looked at me with an expression of genuine affection and vulnerability.

"This bloody manager you have is useless," he said. "He keeps bothering me about providing you money in London so that you can eat food and stay in a hotel." He spat out the words "eat food and stay in a hotel" as if they were synonymous with "buy drugs and visit brothels."

"I know," I said, apologetically, "but if you are sending me to London for the weekend, I am going to need a place to stay."

He stood up and walked to the outer office and returned with a crisp white envelope and a blank sheet of paper. He sat down, took a fountain pen out of the inkwell next to him, and began to write.

"Now, this is what I am proposing. You will stay in my flat while you are in London. I will already be there so I will greet you and I will cook you breakfast. You may tell your bloody manager that the great Ismail Merchant made you omelets every morning as if he was your own personal chef. Secondly, as far as the rest of your food goes, there is a wonderful Indian restaurant down the street from my flat whose owner is my dear friend Mr. Khan."

He read aloud as he wrote, "Dear Mr. Khan, please let my colleague Aasif Mandvi order anything off your menu, and feel free to put it on my tab. Yours sincerely, Ismail Merchant."

He then put the letter into the envelope, sealed it, and gave it to me.

"Remember," he said, "when Mr. Khan presents you with the bill, make sure he is giving me a fifty percent discount."

London was cold, damp, and gray, but Ismail's flat was impeccably decorated with bright colors and fabrics from all over the world. Every piece of furniture seemed to have been brought over from the maharaja's palace in Jaipur or Christie's auction house. Ismail was already there when I arrived and gave me a brief tour of his home. He lingered over many artifacts and paintings, describing their origins in loving detail, but it was clear that his prized possession was the set of antique dining room chairs that he claimed were handmade in Rajasthan in the 1600s.

After the tour, Ismail departed and for most of the two days I stayed in his flat, I hardly saw him. The dining chairs were incredibly uncomfortable but there was nowhere else to sit while eating my takeout from Mr. Khan's. Also, the dining room was the only room with a television, under which was a collection of DVDs, mostly of his own films with a few by Fellini and Satyajit Ray thrown into the mix. While eating samosas, watching *A Room with a View* (which I realized I had never seen), and enjoying the meta experience of watching the Merchant/Ivory aesthetic onscreen while literally sitting in the midst of the Merchant/Ivory aesthetic, I leaned back and felt the seat of the chair come loose from the frame. I had broken his priceless chair.

Shit! In a panic I found some Super Glue in a box in a cupboard down the hall, and attempted to glue it back together. With a few well-placed dollops the chair seemed to be back to its original form and I hoped no would be the wiser. Ismail was flying to Mumbai and I was flying back to New York the next day, so as long as he didn't sit in it, the damaged chair would hopefully go unnoticed until I was long gone.

That evening Ismail came home and announced he would be cooking and having a few guests over for dinner. I could join them if I liked.

A handful of well-dressed people in suits and saris gathered in his dining room later that night and talked of film, food, politics . . . and, of course, Ismail. I walked in to the room inconspicuously, trying to stay out of sight. It didn't work. Ismail caught my eye the moment I entered the room and in mid-conversation turned to his friends.

"Let me introduce you to the next great star of the Merchant/ Ivory family," he said pointing to me. "This young man is the star of my new film *The Mystic Masseur*, also starring the great Om Puri, a wonderful actress named Ayesha Dharkar, and the incomparable James Fox."

The guests turned to me with huge smiles on their faces. Toasts and congratulations were tossed in our direction as Ismail came and stood with his arm on my shoulder. Just as I was reaching to shake the hand of the nearest guest, I saw one of the older ladies in the room sit down on the antique chair that I had glued together. With a shriek and a flying plate of chicken mango curry, basmati rice, and okra, she collapsed amid a pile of three-hundred-year-old hand-crafted wood and plush purple satin.

"He broke my bloody chair!" Ismail screamed, without missing a beat, as he helped the poor woman back to her feet. "He was having sex on my chair, and he broke it!"

I did a double take, not sure if I heard him correctly. I began to deny the preposterous allegation but didn't have a chance as he continued with even more flamboyance and showmanship.

"Unbelievable," he said now with a distinct smile as he helped wipe the yellow and red stain off the poor woman's blouse with some seltzer and a napkin. "See what happens? You extend someone the courtesy of having them stay in your home, you offer to make some-one a movie star for God's sake, and this is how he repays you: by having sex on your antique chair and breaking it."

I could not believe what I was hearing. The great storyteller, who had become one of the most prolific and unlikely Hollywood success stories, was accusing me in front of a group of strangers of having sex on his priceless antique chair. I stood dumbfounded until I realized as everyone turned to me, faces horrified, that this was part of his theater. He was clearly delighting in the deliciousness of serving this lie to his audience as much as he might in serving them his delicious lemon daal. Fiction was better than truth in his world. I smiled. Instead of an embarrassing moment, it became a hilarious moment, even if it was at my expense.

I turned to the guests and played along, taking the cue from my director to be.

"I'm very embarrassed," I apologized.

Ismail looked at his guests and smiled.

"What are you going to do?" he replied. "That's what happens when you let an actor stay in your house. Hugh Grant was worse."

Everyone laughed.

I arrived in Trinidad on December 31st of that same year to begin shooting *The Mystic Masseur*.

Ismail housed me in a lovely home he had rented with a pool and a beautiful garden in Port of Spain, but I was not there to lie by the pool. I arrived armed with my wall charts, my accent tapes, and my books about Trinidad. I had a collection of photographs from the region in the 1950s that I pasted onto my bedroom wall for inspiration.

It was New Year's Eve when we arrived, and after a party that Ismail had thrown for the cast and crew, Om Puri suggested he and I and a local actor with a car go into Port of Spain and check out the bars. Initially I declined, saying I had to go home to study my script and be well-rested for the start of filming.

"Boy," said Om, leaning out of the passenger side window, "you will learn more about how to play this role by drinking with the locals than learning your lines. Trust me, I've made a hundred films."

"Is that true?" I asked, impressed.

"Of course not," said Om. "I've made a hundred and twenty-three. Now get in the car."

The first day of shooting was supposed to start at five A.M., but luckily I got more shut-eye than I expected since the ex-con they had hired to be my driver forgot to show up. A production assistant picked me up at seven, which pushed production to nine. When we arrived, Ismail was running around in the ninety-degree heat screaming at extras and crew like a blur wearing a caftan. Since I had never actually spoken to Ismail about the script or the scenes or anything, I imagined that first he would sit down with me and discuss some things. The first scene I was going to shoot was on a farm road with a wonderful eighty-nine-year-old actress named Zohra Seghal who was playing my grandmother. I assumed we would all have long conversations about our characters' relationship and Ismail's vision of the scene and how it fit into the larger story. As it turned out, I would have had a better chance of going over my scene with one of the local farmers.

This was a passion project for the great producer and what would turn out to be the last of only four movies he would ever direct himself. I realized very quickly, and much to my dismay, that my expectations of starring in my first movie were very different than Ismail's expectations of me starring in my first movie. The luxury of excavating a character or text analysis were left to the safety of Wynn Handman's acting class—that was the process that one is allowed on stage or in grad school, with weeks of rehearsal. This was the world of independent filmmaking; this was the world where Ismail was creating something out of nothing.

The first few days I followed Ismail around with questions that he never answered or he thought were pointless or he answered with a perfunctory, "Sure, fine, try it." He didn't have time to hold my hand, he didn't have time to talk to me about character and the truth of a scene or the legitimacy of dialogue because, well . . . because I realized he didn't know how to. He was in his own process. He was painting the story he wanted to paint, even if sometimes that story was pretending that he knew what he was doing. I started having sleepless nights as I became afraid that without any guidance, without a director who could talk to me, my performance in this film might be the beginning and the end of my career. I was infuriated and disappointed that he seemed to care more about getting an immoveable cow with a rider on it to gallop through the foreground of a scene than answering a single question about the relationship between my character and his grandmother, which happened to be the scene the cow was an extra in.

His filmmaking maddened me. He spent forty-five minutes figuring out how to get the chickens on the roof of the house we were shooting in front of not to walk out of frame during the scene. He finally instructed the Indian boys on the crew to tie the feet of the chickens together and hold the other end of the string just off camera so they literally could not move. As a result the chickens were furious and clucked so loudly they almost drowned out the actors.

Ismail treated the script like a suggestion and every day we would invariably end up shooting scenes that were never written. It confounded me to no end since I had not prepared for them. He would see a wonderful road or a view or a tree that he liked and we would stop and shoot a scene. Once, when told to ride my bicycle down a particular road, I told him that the scene was not in the screenplay.

"Never mind," he said. "I don't care what's in the screenplay. This is a beautiful road and I want to see you riding your bike down it."

"But where is my character even going?" I asked.

"He's going home!" Ismail replied, irritated and impatient to start filming.

"Well, then tell me where I am coming from," I pressed.

"Umm . . ." he said, searching for an answer, "you are coming from Ram Logan's shop."

I paused and then reminded Ismail that didn't make any sense because it was well established in the film that Ram Logan's shop was across the street from my house.

"Maybe you are taking the scenic route!" he screamed. "Now please stop talking and get on the bike and ride."

At another point in filming I was honestly not sure if he was mad or a genius when I saw him instruct crew members to dress up in camouflage with giant leaves, hide in the marshland, and then scare a flock of geese that would fly over a vintage car carrying myself and actor Sanjeev Bhaskar as it drove down a country road. But he got the shot and I could not deny, it was beautiful.

What I came to realize as production went on and I was working sometimes twelve to fourteen hours a day was that this adventure would never be what I wanted it to be. I complained to myself that Ismail was not interested in my creative input and the work I had done on my character. It seemed like I was just a tool to him, a prop, a color on his palette board, and I was not entirely wrong.

One day when I was not called to the set and had planned to have a relaxing day off going over my upcoming scenes, an intern showed up at my front door saying Ismail wanted me on the set ready to shoot.

"What scene?" I asked. "It's my day off."

"I know," he said, "it's not in the script. It's something he added to the schedule this morning."

I was furious as I was pulled from my day to go through hair and makeup and was planted back on set. I felt disrespected and used. I grumbled, complained, and hollered to anyone who would listen (except Ismail), asking how was I supposed to give a worthy performance under these conditions. Om Puri was growing frustrated with my grumbling and finally he lost his patience and said four words that boomed out of his pockmarked face, like it was a megaphone: "Boy, do your work."

This was exactly what I needed to hear, because he was absolutely right. That's all I could do. In the midst of the insanity or magic that was Ismail Merchant, all I could do was my work. Everything else was out of my control. It's also exactly what I was not doing. The charts, the research, worrying about the accent—even though it was all important stuff, I had spent weeks hiding behind it, using it as a crutch, afraid that I was going to be bad, afraid that I was going to fail. I may not have agreed with the way Ismail did things, but what I had to admire was that he was an artist who was not handcuffed by the worry that what he was creating would be viewed as good or bad. He was just creating, often in the moment, without any reason or rationale. He had given me a huge opportunity to do the same and that's what I was blowing. The rest of the shoot was just as frustrating, but slowly I let go of worrying about the work and I managed to just do the work.

The Mystic Masseur premiered the following year in New York City. I was incredibly nervous to see it with an audience. I had heard through other actors and some of the other producers that unfortunately not one single A-list or even B-list celebrity was going to be able to attend the premiere. Woody Allen had a movie opening the same night and Paul Newman was having an event that everyone in New York seemed to be invited to. I was simultaneously disappointed and somewhat relieved.

Ismail called me before the screening and said, "The film is a masterpiece."

I smiled because I knew he was lying.

"There will be lots of press at the premiere, you should be very excited."

I smiled again, because I knew he was lying.

"But no one famous is coming, right?" I asked, hoping that was indeed the case.

"They can have their movie stars," Ismail scoffed. "I have managed to snag the biggest celebrity in the world."

"You have?" I said, wondering if Oprah could actually ruin my career if she hated this movie.

As I stepped out of a limousine with my parents at the premiere, which Ismail had turned into a fundraiser for the American India Foundation, I saw what he meant when the handful of press who had showed up suddenly stopped taking pictures of me and turned their lenses on the biggest celebrity in the world who also happened to be a board member of the American India Foundation: Former President Bill Clinton.

As the film started, I realized that Ismail Merchant had done what he did best. He had told the story the way he saw it. The movie was not perfect; in fact it got tremendously mixed reviews from the people in the theater that night and beyond. It would not go on to do much business at the box office or change my life in the way I thought it would, but as I watched the film, I saw for the first time what my story really was. It was not the story that I was hoping it would be—that of a young actor who gives an Oscar-winning performance his first time out and is applauded as the next great talent of our generation. It was instead the story of a young actor who is given an unbelievable opportunity, not to become a movie star, but to learn how to star in a movie.

Bill Clinton may have stood up and left ten minutes after the film began and gone to Paul Newman's party down the street, but it didn't matter. After the screening was over and people came up to me and my parents and congratulated me on a job well done, I realized that Ismail Merchant had given me something that perhaps no one else could have. He showed me how to make a great story out of a broken chair.

BROOKE AND MONDAY-WALA

BROOKE SHIELDS KICKED ME OUT of her New Year's Eve party and I blame Jenny Cockshot and a very powerful pot brownie. Now, I have never been that guy that people kick out of their parties. It had never happened to me before. I am a fairly decent conversationalist and with the right music I'm a pretty good dancer, so mostly people like having me at their parties.

First of all, let me preface this story by saying that it was perfectly appropriate for Brooke to throw me out of her party. I might have done the same thing in her position. However, the reason this incident was significant was because of my strange history with Brooke Shields. Brooke and I were not friends. In fact, I had never really spoken to her. And yet when I was fourteen years old I went to sleep every night staring into her eyes.

When I was a kid, everyone had posters up in their bedroom. And since it was the seventies, most boys had posters of the scantily-clad Farrah Fawcett or the libido-raising dominatrixy Lynda Carter as Wonder Woman, or in the case of my friend Darren, the tightly-uniformed Erik Estrada. I had only one poster on my bedroom wall. It wasn't even really a poster, it was just a photograph torn out of a magazine. It showed Brooke as a young screen goddess, barely a teenager, with puckered, moist lips, hair blown back, and a sultry expression in her eyes. I had posted the picture on the wall right to next to my pillow, so every night just before I turned off my lamp, Brooke was the last face I would see. She was the girl with whom I imagined I could go see movies. A beautiful girlfriend to hold my hand. Someone I could talk to.

I was too young to have seen any of her movies (although I had seen the trailers and I was determined that *Blue Lagoon* would be the first movie I would rent as soon as I turned sixteen) and her famous Calvin Klein ads had somehow never made it across the Atlantic, so I became aware of Brooke mostly because of an interview that I saw on TV one night.

She was a child star, appearing before the cameras to promote a film. I was instantly captivated by her. She was beautiful, but my attraction came from more than that. She, like me, seemed sad and alone. I had recently discovered my passion for acting and even though she was a glamorous Hollywood movie star who lived in a world very different than that of an Indian kid whose father had a corner shop in a Pakistani ghetto in the north of England, I was sure that if we ever did meet, we would have an instant connection.

My real-life Brooke was a girl named Jenny Cockshot. I had secretly been in love with Jenny since I had arrived at Mandale Middle School. She was very real, but just as unattainable. Her lips, her teeth, her eyes, her training bra: all of it was perfect. She used to wear sexy white turtlenecks that made her seem regal. I had never spoken to her either—she walked around school on the arm of a young tough guy named Brian.

In the showers after P.E. I couldn't help but notice that Brian had perfectly developed biceps, real honest-to-goodness biceps. I had never seen such huge biceps before, but his dad was a builder and I figured Brian probably spent his summers building houses. However, that failed to explain his giant penis. I had never seen a penis that large before, either. Everything about Brian was larger than me and standing next to him in the showers made me feel like a stick figure.

It seemed that Brian's biceps, his penis size, and the fact that he was handsome and white gave him a sense of entitlement to do whatever to whomever he felt like. Once during P.E., Brian's friend Justin caught me staring at Jenny while we were supposed to be climbing ropes. Brian had easily climbed to the top of his rope with biceps bulging while I spun around entangled at the bottom of mine like it was a maypole.

"Hey, Brian," Justin yelled across the gym. "I think Monday-wala fancies your Jenny."

(Mandviwala was too difficult for the kids to pronounce, so they called me Monday-wala. Since I never objected and instead played it off like I thought it was hilarious, soon I was not only called Monday-wala, but Tuesday-wala, Wednesday-wala, etc., depending on the day of the week. I heard it so often that I once failed to recognize my real last name during roll call. The teacher stood at the front of the room for a good fifteen seconds just saying my name in a flat monotonous tone, "Mandviwala. Mandviwala. Mandviwala." It wasn't until one of the other students laughed and reminded the confused teacher it was Thursday that I perked up and paid attention.)

As soon as Justin yelled, I panicked and averted my gaze from Jenny's direction. My eyes darted around the gym like I was possessed.

"No, I don't," I protested, feigning laughter.

Jenny shot me a look that was a mixture of confusion and outrage from across the gym, which sent me into another panic.

"I mean not that I wouldn't, I just meant . . ." I mumbled apologetically in her direction. I looked up and saw Brian hanging atop the ropes watching me silently like a bird of prey.

The bus ride home that afternoon was tense. Brian taunted me from the back with his arm around Jenny.

"Hey Monday-wala, look at me," he called. "Hey, look at me, you wog. You like my girl? You like my Jenny? You want my Jenny?"

The city bus was always filled with a dozen or so riotous kids that the bus driver yelled at all the way home, but that day felt different. Except for Brian's taunting the rest of the bus was silent. I turned for a moment and saw Jenny laughing with her head on his shoulder as Brian threw a half-eaten sandwich in my direction.

As soon as the bus came to my stop, at the top of Great Horton Road, I jumped up, grabbed my school bag, and ran. I heard Brian screaming as he and three others followed in hot pursuit. I dodged traffic and went slamming through manicured bushes, trampling flowers in strange backyards.

"Don't you ever look at my girlfriend, you fuckin' wog!" he yelled as he gained on me. "Don't you ever look at her again."

I ran down the hill. My school bag tangled between my legs, threatening to trip me up. But before Brian could catch me, I turned and ducked into a back alley, jumped over a wall, and ran down past the reservoir to the back of our subdivision and over the fence into my own backyard to safety. I walked into my bedroom exhausted, my pants ripped, my arms and face covered in dirt, and there she was. Looking at me with that puckered mouth and those soft-focus eyes as if to say, "Don't worry. Those guys are assholes. I like you. Go get yourself a peanut butter sandwich and a glass of milk and come lay next to me and make up a conversation that we might have if we actually knew each other."

A few years later my parents made the monumental decision to leave our life in the UK and move to Tampa, Florida. I remembered that in some teen magazine I had read that Brooke lived in a place known for its lavish gardens. A place called New Jersey. I imagined her walking through gardens and meadows every day with flowers in her hands like she was a character in some BBC period drama. I pulled out a map and saw that New Jersey was actually quite far from Tampa and not a place that I could probably go to on my own. However, the state itself seemed small, and conceivably if we lived there, I would most likely run into Brooke at the grocery store or maybe we would even go to the same school.

I decided to make a heartfelt campaign for us to move not to Florida but instead to New Jersey, much to my parents' confusion.

"What's wrong with you, beta?" my father asked after I made my pitch. "You will love Florida. They have sunshine, beaches, and even Disney World."

I was too embarrassed to admit the truth, so I replied, "I don't like beaches, I like gardens."

My father looked at my mother and said, "This is what happens when you allow your son to do theater."

Needless to say, we didn't move to New Jersey and soon the image of the girl on my wall faded into the distant past only to be rekindled by a moment many years later when, having pursued my dream of being an actor, I lived in New York City and worked as a waiter for one of New York's finest catering companies. One of the events that I worked at one year was the NBC upfront party, where the network would announce its upcoming season. All the network stars were there, and as I stood by the door in my tuxedo surveying the room, I suddenly spotted "Suddenly Susan" herself, Brooke Shields, amid a gaggle of paparazzi and admirers. As I stared at her from across the room, it all came flooding back: the nights I went to sleep staring at her face, the fantasy that someday I would get back at Brian by having Brooke Shields be my girlfriend, and the dream of wanting to live in New Jersey. Fifteen years earlier I would have given my right arm to be standing exactly where I was in that moment.

It was as if the preteen inside of me was screaming, "Oh my God, it's her! Oh my God, it's her! Come on, let's go over there. Just make an excuse to walk over to her."

"No, I am staying right here," I told myself. "I'm an adult now. That was a long time ago and I'm not going to act like some crazy teen fanboy."

"Are you insane?" my middle school self shot back. "Standing ten feet away is the girl of your childhood dreams! At least walk by and make eye contact. It may be the only chance you ever get."

Just as my inner argument was reaching its peak, Brooke suddenly looked away from the flashing lenses and microphones, turned and locked eyes with me. She smiled. It was surreal. Brooke Shields was smiling at me and I know this sounds crazy but it was as if she had been looking for me and was relieved to have finally found me after all these years. My middle school self was absolutely elated, saying, "She remembers. She remembers!" while my adult self stood in complete shock. As if things couldn't get any stranger, a moment later she lifted her hand and beckoned me forward. Was I dreaming? Could this really be happening right now? My middle school self seemed to push me forward and I floated toward her with a strange grin on my face.

As I reached her she put her arm on my shoulder, leaned down, and whispered, ever so softly, "You are the man I have been looking for. Could you please get me a glass of red wine?"

I blushed and nodded as I scurried away to do her bidding, then returned a few seconds later and handed her a glass of cabernet, reminding my middle school self that he should not be too disappointed. Brooke Shields did softly touch my arm, look into my eyes, look down at my name tag and say, "Thank you Asaaf." I mean, she said my name . . . kind of. But I could sense that middle school me was not satisfied and secretly hoped that he and Brooke would be in the same room again for a do-over. Ten years later, it happened.

It was the night before New Year's Eve. I went out to dinner with my friend Carol, who is a very beautiful and successful actress in her own right. Carol knew the chef at this particular restaurant and so we were both curious about what unique appetizer he would prepare for us. The chef, a buoyant energetic fellow, came bounding out of the kitchen with a grin on his face soon after we sat down. We talked about the menu and before he went back to the kitchen he said he had something special for us. I was excited to see what gastronomical delight he would come back with. To my surprise he returned with two small discs wrapped in tinfoil, and sheepishly handed them to us.

"These are my gift to you, to enjoy," he said. "Take them tomorrow night before midnight and have an amazing New Year's Eve."

Inside were two beautifully constructed pot brownies. Carol looked at me.

"Will you try it?" she asked.

"My first pot brownie," I replied. "I will if you will."

We both agreed that we would take them wherever we were the next night and then meet up. I fantasized a little about the idea that perhaps we would meet up in some alternate pot-brownie-high universe where inhibitions might be discarded and for a moment she would forget that she didn't think of me "that way."

The next night a group of South Asian friends and I decided to see a play called *Fuerza Bruta* in Union Square. The show is designed to overstimulate, immersing the audience into the action of the theatrical experience. It has a pulsating soundtrack, strobe lights, and an underwater acrobatics show above your head (seriously, look it up), so of course it would be the perfect show to see after eating a pot brownie. In fact, I am willing to bet the show was conceived after someone had eaten a pot brownie . . . or ten.

The show ran its full course and my brownie never kicked in. I was truly disappointed. After the show, since it was only nine-thirty, we decided to get some sushi at a nearby restaurant. While waiting for our tables, it happened, hard. I no longer knew if I was dreaming or awake, if my legs were incredibly long or the ground was on a very steep angle, and it seemed that I couldn't change my expression. I sat all throughout dinner with a ridiculous shit-eating grin on my face, convinced that I was unable to change my muscular formation.

Inside, I was terrified and all I could do was keep telling everyone that I was "weally, weally wowied awout my face." My friends laughed and carried on because from their perspective my huge grin seemed to indicate that I was "weally, weally" enjoying myself.

After dinner we went to a club. The music was loud, I had a garland around my neck, a hat that said 2011, and was trying to decide what geometric shape the human hand was. That's when the phone rang. It was Carol. I walked outside the club to take the call.

"Where are you?" she asked.

"At a club," I said. "Where are you?"

"I'm at Brooke Shields' New Year's party at her apartment. Why don't you come? Brooke said she would be thrilled to have you come over."

Now I am going to assume it was the pot brownie that allowed for this to happen, but my younger, middle-school version of myself suddenly popped out of my head through my eyeballs and was standing right next to me, plain as day, unable to truly comprehend what he had just heard and was running around screaming.

"Yes! Yes! Yes! Did Brooke Shields just say she would be thrilled to have me come over? Are you kidding me? Why are we still on the phone? Tell her you are on your way. Get the address and let's dump these guys and go. Come on, man, get the address, let's go!"

"I can't do that," I said to both him and Carol on the phone. "I'm with a group of people, it would be rude to just leave."

"What? I can hardly hear you," came her response.

"I'M WITH SOME FRIENDS!" I yelled over the din of the music and the New Year's traffic and drunken revelers.

"Sure, bring them," she yelled back, "I'm sure it will be fine."

Now, while young Aasif literally went dancing out into the street screaming, "Who the man? WE the man! Who the man? WE the man!" I sat my extremely long legs and oddly-shaped hands down on the sidewalk in a sweat-drenched, stoned, dreamlike trance and reminded myself that even though tomorrow I might discover that this was all a hallucination, right now I was going to remain coherent and marvel at the strangeness of life.

The pin-up I had on my wall as a child had just invited me to be a guest at her home. Wow. I assumed it was because she knew me from *The Daily Show*. After all these years I would finally speak to the girl on my wall as an equal. We would be friends. What a moment. My do-over was about to happen.

After we left the club I told my friends that we had been invited to Brooke Shields' New Year's Eve party. They were game to go, though they had to make a beer stop on the way. I told them I would meet them there, giving them the address and hailing a cab.

Upon arriving at Brooke's apartment I was met by her husband, who invited me in. The scene I walked in to was quite different than the one I had imagined. This was a champagne and hors d'oeuvres-style intimate dinner party with about two dozen of Brooke's friends. Carol spotted me across the room and waved me over.

"Happy New Year! How was the brownie?" she asked.

"Horrible," I said. "I've been smiling for the last three hours."

She looked confused; I told her I would explain later. I wanted to meet Brooke and thank her for inviting me. Suddenly, there she was, standing by the buffet speaking to a friend. Young Aasif started dragging me over to her, saying, "Letsgoletsgo!" But this time I told him to shut up and sit down; the grown-ups were talking.

I excused myself and walked across the apartment toward her. She had not made eye contact with me yet, but just like that night many years ago at the NBC upfronts event I was sure that she would look up in the next moment and wave me over. Only this time it would not be about getting her a glass of wine.

Then the buzzer rang.

I stopped in my tracks. I turned and saw Brooke's husband greeting a hodgepodge motley crew of sweaty, stoned, drunk brown people as they tumbled into the apartment, laughing and singing, wearing New Year's Eve hats and blowing noisemakers. My friends had arrived.

I turned and marched toward them to warn them that perhaps we had miscalculated the tone of this party and that maybe they should in some way bring it down a notch or two, but I was too late. My friends raided the buffet table, stuffing mini quiches in their mouths and grabbing handfuls of chocolate truffles and sushi. One even dared to raid Brooke herself, taking selfies with her and telling her what a huge fan he was of her work, at a decibel level that ensured the rest of her guests knew it as well.

I stood paralyzed in the middle of the floor, wanting to talk to Brooke but also wanting to disappear, as what seemed like a drunken Bollywood wedding party invaded this mostly Caucasian, patrician cocktail reception. I had a dreadful premonition that I had made a terrible mistake by coming here and was gripped with an unsettling conspicuousness that made me retreat toward the door. Food was being eaten, pictures were being taken, loudness and drunkenness abounded until after a few minutes Carol appeared by my side with an apologetic expression.

"Umm . . . I'm sorry, this might have been a bad idea," she began. "Brooke doesn't know these people and she doesn't feel comfortable having all these strangers in her home. She told me to tell you that you are welcome to stay, but your friends, unfortunately . . ."

"I completely understand," I said, cutting her off. I looked at Brooke as she stood by the buffet table in mid-conversation and I looked at my friends, who were stuffing their faces with cupcakes.

"But I want to stay," I heard young Aasif say. "I don't want to leave. It's Brooke Shields! The girl on your wall, remember? And she invited you to her house. We've arrived."

I looked between the elegant Brooke and my disheveled friends.

Suddenly I felt the sting of a half-eaten sandwich hit me on the side of the face. With it came a familiar voice that I had not heard in many years.

"Yeah, get out Monday-wala," Brian called to me from across the room as he stepped out from behind the curtains. "You and your curry-breathing friends don't belong here. Pathetic little Monday-wala, still getting chased away and still can't get the girl. Boo-hoo."

"Shut up, you wanker!" I heard young Aasif scream, as he charged at Brian from across the room and leapt on him, throwing him against the buffet table. I had a momentary heart attack as I watched the two of them careen around the living room, punching and kicking each other until it became clear to me that no one else was seeing what I was seeing. Just as I vowed that I would never eat another pot brownie ever again, Carol suddenly came back into focus.

"Aasif," she said, "did you hear me? I'm sorry. Your friends need to go."

"It's totally cool," I said calmly, watching the melee no one else could see. "We're all gonna go."

I gathered up my friends, in some cases taking stuffed pastries and deviled eggs out of their hands and mouths and ushered us all to the door. As I walked out, I looked over to where Brooke was standing, but she was nowhere to be found. I had an impulse to go search for her and explain myself, but I didn't. Instead I stepped into the elevator with my posse and went down to the street.

Unfazed by the experience and still wanting to party, my friends talked about how the night was still young and where we should go next. I walked silently for a few blocks until I saw younger Aasif standing on a street corner. His hair was a mess, his lip was bleeding, he had a black eye and his clothes were torn.

"How'd you do?" I asked him, smiling.

"I kicked his ass," he said.

"Good for you," I replied.

"Did you get to talk to Brooke?" he asked.

"No."

"Bummer," he said.

"Not really," I replied putting my arm around him. "Turns out, there was nothing I needed to say."

THE JIHADIST OF IRONY

"Is this Jon Stewart fellow crazy? How can he hire a guy who doesn't even know how to do a proper salaam to his parents to be his senior bloody Muslim correspondent?"

"It's a comedy show, Dad."

"I hope so," my father said. "Is he expecting you to be funny?"

"Yes," I said defensively. "Why is that so hard to believe? I've done a lot of comedy. You saw me do street improvisational comedy when I worked at Disney MGM Studios. I was in a very successful sketch comedy group in New York and remember on Broadway when I did *Oklahoma!*? I was hilarious as the peddler."

"Beta, we loved you in *Oklahoma!*," my mother chimed in on the other line. "Don't listen to your father. You were very funny in that. The scenery was amazing. It was incredible. You really felt like you were *in* Oklahoma."

I sighed.

"Remember this," my father continued. "If Jon Stewart asks you any questions or your opinion about Islam, don't you say a word, just have him call your mother, she knows everything."

"Yes, beta," agreed my mom. "Just tell him to call me, because you don't want to say the wrong thing on television and then get your entire family in trouble."

"Don't humiliate your entire family!" continued my dad. "Otherwise we will be a laughingstock from here to Mumbai. By the way, congratulations! This is very exciting. We are very proud of you!"

The day that I became the senior Middle East/Muslim/All Things Brown correspondent on *The Daily Show* was just like any other day. Kind of. It began with me sitting in the park with my laptop writing a letter to my ex-girlfriend who I had recently found out was engaged. I had been in a miserable funk about the engagement for about a week, and when I say funk I mean not eating and listening to Ben Harper's "Another Lonely Day" on an iTunes loop. Sometimes I would talk to friends who would listen to me go on about my pathological inability to truly commit to someone who loved me, which would then launch me into singing Ben Harper's "Another Lonely Day." The letter I was writing was incredibly cathartic. It felt deep and meaningful and said all the things I had never said when we were together. It was the kind of letter that I knew my ex would probably skim through and then throw away, because she had not been living in denial for the past year, had actually moved on, and didn't want to explain to her fiancé why her ex-boyfriend was writing a ten-page letter to her a year after their breakup.

Then my cell phone rang. It was my manager's assistant.

"*The Daily Show* is looking for someone who looks Middle Eastern," he said. "Do you want to go down and read for them?"

Well, here we go again, I thought to myself. Even though this sounded like it could be some bizarre Homeland Security sting operation, I knew what it really was. This would be no different than that time I was the voice of Saddam Hussein on the David Letterman show or the time I played a tech support agent from Bangalore for Jimmy Kimmel. I knew if I said yes to this, my day would end with me either wearing a fake beard yelling, "Death to America!" or worse still, wearing a turban, sitting on a carpet, and pretending to fly.

Filled with a surprising fortitude and a devil-may-care attitude that was no doubt the direct result of heartbreak, I said, "Tell *The Daily Show* to go fuck themselves." And hung up the phone.

It rang again a few minutes later.

"Actually, they would like you to come in and read for the role of a correspondent," my manager's assistant said when I finally picked up.

I thought about this for a moment. I had watched *The Daily Show*, I was a fan, but even though I had done a lot of comedy, I mostly associated it with stand-up types. I was a real actor, I thought to myself. I had cut my teeth on Chekhov, Ibsen, and Shakespeare. *The Daily Show* seemed like the last place I wanted to be.

"Well, I am very sad today," I said. "I don't think I can be funny. Perhaps I can go in another day. You see, I found out my ex just got engaged and I am in the middle of writing a heart-wrenching—"

"Sorry," he interrupted, "I have another call coming in, but they are only seeing people until three today, what time should I tell them you will be there?"

"Two forty-five," I said.

Three hours later I walked into *The Daily Show* building. After a brief wait I was called in to the studio. Jon Stewart stood up from behind his desk wearing jeans and a sweatshirt, shook my hand, and introduced himself.

"Thanks for coming down," he said.

"Of course," I replied. "I'm a big fan of the show."

"We tape the show in front of a live audience," he continued, sounding somewhat concerned. "Have you ever performed before a live audience before?"

"I've been on Broadway," I responded, eager to let him know that he was getting prime "actor" rib, not some cheap flank steak.

"Oh, great," he responded. "Well, let's do this, then. Just stand on your mark and look into the teleprompter and here we go."

"Do you want me to do an accent?" I asked.

"No, no," Jon replied. "We don't need an accent. I don't think we need an accent. Just as you are."

This was something brown actors don't hear all that often when auditioning for television so I was pleasantly surprised, even though I had been practicing my go-to generic Middle Eastern accent for the last fifteen minutes in the green room. Instead, consummate professional that I am, I thought, "Fuck it, I'm just gonna impersonate Stephen Colbert." I cocked my eyebrow, assumed a rather arched comic tone and spoke with faux seriousness as I said the words that came up on the teleprompter.

Jon stood up from his desk and turned to me after the audition. He was smiling from ear to ear.

"Welcome to *The Daily Show*!" he said. "Do you have plans this evening? We tape at six."

That was it. At first I thought I might be part of a weird *Daily Show* gotcha prank, since jobs don't usually happen like that, and to be fair I spent the next several months in trial mode until they offered me an official contract. But in that moment, just like that, I became the Gupta/Zakaria/Velshi/Amanpour masala on the *Daily Show* smorgasbord, which at that point mostly consisted of white people. More significantly, however, I also brought the halal factor by becoming *The Daily Show*'s ironically named "senior Muslim correspondent." This was all in spite of the fact that I was a terrible example of a Muslim and knew nothing about the news except what I learned from watching *The Daily Show*. The last thing I had any knowledge of was how to be a "Muslim comedy journalist person."

I spent the first year on the show convinced that I was the wrong guy for the job and that they would soon discover they had made a terrible mistake. I flashed forward to the end of my career and saw the highlight reel run through my mind: *Aasif Mandvi played more doctors than any other actor in the history of American cinema but the pinnacle of his career came when he was fired by Jon Stewart.*

But after some time I became aware of the fact that people seemed to be responding positively to what I was doing on the show and something started happening that had never happened to me before: I began getting shout-outs on the streets. I was living on the Upper West Side of Manhattan at the time, so it was mostly liberal Jews, unless I went downtown, where it was NYU students and the occasional hipster wearing a top hat riding a skateboard. This wasn't so odd in and of itself—it kind of comes with the territory. But then brown people started to recognize me: Indians, Pakistanis, Arabs, and Muslims. Muslims began to come up to me on the street and would say things like, "Thank you for what you are doing," "Keep it up," or worse still, "A salaam alaikum."

My experience with Muslims before this was mostly at my parents' mosque, where, judged for my spouseless-actor-in-New-York lifestyle, everyone treated me as if I had a bottle of whiskey in my sock and a pig for a best friend. But now, suddenly, Muslims began to treat me as if I was one of their own. They wanted to hug me; they wanted to tell me how using satire to address the issues of the Middle East and the war on terror on *The Daily Show* was oftentimes more effective than the work they were doing through the "Islam Anti-Defamation League." They also wanted to know if I was married, because they would like to introduce me to their daughter.

It all made me incredibly uncomfortable for two reasons. Firstly, I realized that they thought I was like them and I was not. My relationship with Islam was complicated and contentious. I had taken great delight in arguing with conservative Muslims who would tell me crazy shit like, "Eating pork will make you want to sleep with your mother," or in provoking imams by telling them that they could learn as much about the human condition by reading Rumi or Shakespeare as they could from reading the Koran. I rarely went to the mosque, I never fasted, and I only prayed *namaaz* on the holy nights because my mom bugged me about it.

The second reason it made me uncomfortable was that I liked it. I liked knowing that what I got to say on the show, even though I didn't always write it, was having an impact. Not in terms of policy, or to lawmakers, but to Muslims in America. The fact that there was a brown person, openly identified as Muslim, on national television, talking about the relationship between America and the Muslim world from a vastly underrepresented point of view was a big deal for them. That that brown person happened to be me was absurdly bananas but it started to make me feel, dare I say . . . Muslimy. The whole thing was very unsettling.

The longer I spent time on *The Daily Show* standing in front of a green screen pretending to report from war zones and hot spots around the world—most often from somewhere in the Middle East—the more I began to realize that *The Daily Show* was radicalizing me. I was being allowed to express the outrage that had lain dormant in me since the aftermath of September 11. I was becoming a terrorist of comedy. This was my joke madrasa run mostly by Ivy League-educated Jews, and I was being taught how to commit a jihad of irony against the bullshit, the hypocrisy, the ignorance. I was learning to fire missiles of satire across the basic cable airwaves and blow the minds of a million people. Sometimes we even got up to two million if it was election time. I was able to retaliate on behalf of a sector of society that needed to know that someone, kind of, sort of, had the balls that no one on FOX or CNN had. American Muslims, whether they were religious practitioners or whether, like me, they mostly identified with Islam from a cultural standpoint, had not been allowed the luxury of being both patriotic and critical of America at the same time.

This was evidenced by the brown-faced cabbies on the streets of New York who had adorned their yellow cabs with so much red, white, and blue that they looked like floats in the Fourth of July parade. Anyone with a thick Middle Eastern or South Asian accent quickly replaced *Inshallah* with *God Bless America*.

"Even though on the outside I may look like those that did you harm, I am not one of them," they were attempting to say. "I get that you are angry and afraid but if we just connect for a moment, you will see that I'm actually Armenian or Sikh or from Poughkeepsie. And if I do happen to be Muslim, I am not that freedom-hating type of Muslim. I believe in peace, and baseball. My blood runs apple pie so you can pass over me. Oh ye angel of freedom, liberty, and ignorant racially-driven outrage, pass over me."

Inshall—I mean God Bless America.

My tenure at *The Daily Show* started during the decade after September 11 and fear of Muslims was at an all-time high. Politicians and the media seemed to dial the fright, mistrust, and animosity up to a fever pitch to gain votes and ratings. From supposed experts on the mainstream news reporting absurdities like the spelling of the Muslim holiday of Eid written backward spells *die*, as if Islam was a Led Zeppelin album imbued with backward satanic messages. Or that the definition of jihad has something to do with "death to America," even though Mohammad (PBUH) was born a thousand years before Columbus and if this was true, it would be the mother of all pre-emptive strikes. Or that everyone in India eats chilled monkey brains for dessert (okay fine, that was from *Indiana Jones and the Temple of Doom*, but honestly it had been bothering me since the mid-eighties). To the coverage of less absurd and more dangerous stuff like the Ground Zero mosque protests or proposals that all young Muslim men's names be put into a database, as if they were pedophiles, or the fact that mosques were being infiltrated by undercover informants hired by the NYPD to spy on Muslims who had committed the crime of simply being Muslim. My point is, I was never short of a story to pitch.

I spoke to a woman who was protesting the building of a mosque in Murfreesboro, Tennessee because she believed that it was a terrorist training camp. She also said one in five Muslims are terrorists. I told her that amounted to almost three hundred million terrorists. She didn't balk until I said, "Well, I can't understand what is taking us so long."

I spoke to a young cartoonist who was upset that Marvel was creating a Muslim Batman. When asked why this bothered him, he said, "How can you trust him? He might say he is good but what if he is not?" I felt the need to inform him that Batman was a fictional character in a fictional world created by cartoonists, to which he replied, ". . . exactly, and since there are no Muslims in that fictional world, he shouldn't be there." It was impossible to argue with that kind of air-tight logic. I mean impossible.

I spoke to a panel of New Yorkers who had just watched a parody sitcom we had created based on the idea of a Muslim Cosby show called *The Q'usoby Show*. One gentleman said he could not believe it was a real family. I asked him how we might make it more real. He thought for a second and then said, "What if they had a terrorist uncle who lived in the basement with a goat? Then it would be more believable." Like I said, impossible to argue with.

As the years went by, I can honestly say I began to feel a vague sense of accomplishment by highlighting the absurd and ridiculous. To add fuel to my self-congratulatory fire I was soon being given awards by Muslim organizations for my work. In 2011 I was invited to receive a "Courage in Media" award from the Council on American Islamic Relations. I flew out to California, then got picked up in a limousine and driven to the award show where I was to be honored essentially for making fun of racists and Islamaphobes. As I sat at my table with the other recipients eating my radicchio salad, I got to talking to the young man next to me.

"What's your name?" I asked.

"Malek Jandali," he replied. "I'm a pianist from Syria."

"And what award are you receiving?" I asked.

"The Freedom of Expression Award," he answered. "You?"

"Courage in Media," I laughed. "Honestly, these awards sound a bit overzealous, don't they? I mean, what did you do? Dress up like Lady Gaga in the middle of Damascus?"

He gave me an odd look.

"Over the summer I performed at a rally in Washington, D.C. in support of the Syrian opposition," he explained, "and because of that the Syrian army invaded my family's home in Damascus and brutally beat my parents."

"Okay, then . . ." I stuttered, tasting the dirty leather of the foot that was in my mouth. "See now . . . that's exactly the kind of thing . . . I mean, that's the very definition of . . . I mean good for you . . . I mean not that it was good . . . but you know . . . the thing you did was . . ."

My voice trailed off as I tried not to make eye contact.

"What do you do?" he asked, earnestly.

"Umm . . . Me?" I said. "I'm a smart-ass."

He stared at me with a blank expression. I smiled awkwardly, buttered my bread, and wished that the Syrian army would come and shoot me.

After Jandali received his award, there was not a dry eye in the house. That was followed by my award, which was introduced with a video of me doing pratfalls and making faces into the camera. I stepped up on to the stage, received my award, then went to hug the hijabi woman who gave me the award, forgetting that conservative Muslim women don't hug strange men, and then proceeded to do a stand-up set that they had asked me to perform.

The audience seemed to be amused, even though given the context I felt like I was personally undeserving. I realized, though, as I stood on that stage and did jokes about being racially profiled at airports and Americans being unable to tell the difference between a Mosque and a Mexican restaurant, that this was not really about me. Who I really actually was, personally, was irrelevant. They were not giving this award to *me*. They were giving this award to something that existed in a larger cultural context. I was the representative of an underrepresented character who looked and talked like me but was not really me. He was the creation and the handiwork of myself and many smart funny people: the jihadist of irony.

A few months after that award was given to me, my role as the mouthpiece for that character came into even starker relief when I received a call on my cell phone from Jon Stewart. Jon had never called me before and at first I didn't even recognize his voice.

"I have a question for you," he said. "Trey Parker and Matt Stone showed an image of Mohammad in a bear suit on South Park the other night and they are now being threatened by some Islamic website. I want to do something on the show in response. Can we have an image of Mohammad on the show?"

"No," I said. I didn't even have to think about it. "Definitely not!"

I didn't say no because I was scared. I said it because it felt too easy, too incendiary.

"You're right," said Jon. "Fine. Can we have Jesus on the show?"

"Sure," I said, "Jesus loves the camera."

"Or," said Jon, thinking for a moment, "how would you feel about talking? We do a chat at the desk and I just talk to you about how you personally feel? As a Muslim. Would you be okay doing that?"

My parents' words came back to haunt me: *If Jon Stewart asks you any questions about your opinion on Islam, don't say a word, just have them call your mother.*

I was unsettled and a little terrified.

"Can I call my mother?" I asked.

"Umm . . . sure, whatever you have to do," said Jon. "Let me know."

Later that day, I sat at the desk of *The Daily Show* wearing my suit, in front of an audience about to go on air. Jon leaned over and said, "Thanks for doing this, I know you were hesitant about it."

"You know, Jon," I replied, "it's just that I'm not really a very good example of a Muslim and I can't speak for all of Islam."

"I know," said Jon, as the music began and the stage manager counted us down, "but right now . . . you're all we've got."

ACKNOWLEDGMENTS

I WISH TO THANK the numerous people who made this book possible. The friends and colleagues who I cannot repay, who gave me their time and their ears as they listened to me obsessively read my stories again and again and again. Often the same story. Often the same friends. Whether it was at a formal reading, a writers' workshop, in their homes, in their cars, over the phone, in the emergency room, or at their children's birthday parties, they listened and they shared with me their thoughts, even if that was simply to say, "Aasif, seriously, you cannot just ignore a restraining order." I recognize that some of those friends no longer speak to me, and they will probably never read this acknowledgment, but I still wish to thank them here, for they were paramount in helping me create this book.

I would like to offer a special thanks to my editor Emily Haynes for her tireless work and putting up with me missing every *sodding* deadline. And thanks to Neil Egan and Gregg Kulick for the beautiful jacket and book design, despite having to work with a photograph of me as the raw material. Also to Leigh Haber for helping me begin this process and believing that I had a book inside me. Thank you to my wonderful manager Lillian LaSalle for her commitment, encouragement, and friendship, to my amazing agent Bonnie Bernstein for her support and guidance on this and everything else, and to my literary agents Jennifer Joel and Andrea Barzvi who masterfully put all the pieces together.

On a more personal note, I would like to thank Shaifali Puri for holding my hand and never letting me doubt. Also Jill Anderson, Siddhartha Khosla, Ayad Akhtar, Janina Gavankar, Jim Wisniewski Ruma Bose, Sheetal Sheth, and Nimitt Mankad for their inspiration, wisdom, creativity, and friendship.

Thank you to all the people, too many to name, upon whom the characters in this book are based. In many cases I have changed your names, but you know who you are and I thank you for being part of the story and your teaching along the way.

Finally, I would like to thank Shabana Churruca, Jose Churruca, and Anisa Churruca who continue to teach me the meaning of family, and of course my eternal gratitude to my parents Hakim Mandviwala and the late Fatima Mandviwala, my source material, who always allowed me turn their lives into art and who never compromised their love.